BECOMING A PRIMARY SCHOOL TEACHER
A STUDY OF MATURE WOMEN

Diane Duncan

First published in 1999 by Trentham Books Limited

Trentham Books Limited
Westview House
734 London Road
Oakhill
Stoke on Trent
Staffordshire
England ST4 5NP

British Cataloguing in Publication Data
A catalogue record for this book is available from the
British Library
ISBN 1 85856 104 3
(hb ISBN 1 85856 148 5)

Designed and typeset by Trentham Print Design Ltd., Chester and
printed in Great Britain by Bell & Bain Ltd., Glasgow.

CONTENTS

*For my grandmother Daisy, whose courage, love and vibrant
sense of humour has been a source of lifelong inspiration.*

Acknowledgements

My sincere thanks are extended to the women in this study who admitted me
to their lives and gave so generously of their time. I am especially grateful to
Ann, Linda, Pat, Pamela, Helen, Karen and Christine who found time in their
busy teaching schedules to allow me to interview them yet again. This book
could not have been written without them. Special thanks go to my parents
Joan and Len for their love and unshakeable faith in education; to Marilyn,
Jeanne and Derek for reading and commenting helpfully on draft chapters and
most of all to Colin whose steadfast belief in this project sustained me
throughout.

I am also grateful to the Education Department at the University of Hertford-
shire for providing internal research funding to enable me to bring this book
to completion.

Foreword

With education at the top of the government's agenda and a personal pledge by the Prime Minister to increase participation rates in higher education, we are likely to see many students joining universities and colleges who come from families with little experience of this sector of education. In these circumstances, many things that are taken for granted by students from families who have been through higher education remain as unanswered questions for others. While this is the case for many students, it is especially so for those entering teacher training who have traditionally been drawn from lower social class groups.

Among the questions posed are: What do I need to do to gain entry to a primary teacher training course? What strategies can be developed to revise for examinations? What is it like on teaching practice and how do I get a job? While these questions are not new to those intent on becoming a teacher, it has not always been easy to find answers.

Sources of information often come through general student guides, books devoted to study skills and specific volumes on training to teach. While each of these accounts offer useful advice, it usually comes from senior academics, headteachers, and experts in careers guidance. One voice is absent in all of this – the trainee teacher.

Diane Duncan's book fills a gap by blending together expert advice with accounts drawn from a study of mature women training to be teachers. In these circumstances, we get a vivid portrait of the hopes, fears, highs, lows, doubts and ambitions of trainee teachers in their own words.

This volume is therefore essential reading for all those intending to become primary teachers as it offers much useful advice together with comments from real students. Diane Duncan has provided an insight into the student experience and an essential guide on how to set about becoming a primary school teacher. It deserves to be widely read and should be placed on every reading list for trainee teachers.

Robert Burgess, Vice Chancellor, University of Leicester

Introduction

My work with students over many years has convinced me that they need a book which offers practical guidance on how to succeed as a student teacher, get a job and prepare for the first year of teaching. My research on how mature women experienced their training course revealed some compelling human stories which were worth sharing. The result is a book which gives explicit advice as well as personal accounts of women who know what it means to juggle family responsibilities with a full-time, vocational degree course.

While this book has been written mainly for women contemplating or beginning teacher training there is much which is relevant to men and younger recruits. Tutors will also find useful material and some revealing insights about student perspectives. Most importantly, the book gives hope and encouragement to the legions of women who have the potential to become valued teachers but still hover at the edge of professional training.[1]

The research

I studied twenty-five mature women who were aged between 24 and 45 years when they enrolled on a four-year course at a well-established college of higher education. I was their admissions tutor, education tutor, researcher and woman friend; each role putting me in a strong position to follow their progress. They came with a variety of life and work experiences which included careers in accountancy, banking, social work, computing and nursing. But what they had in common was diverse experience of paid and voluntary work in schools such as parent-helpers, school governors, dining-room helpers and classroom assistants. It was often this kind of contact with children and teachers in schools which had been the catalyst in their decision to train for teaching. In order to get as close as possible to the changes which took place as they adjusted to the role of student teacher, I followed them through their first year of training knowing that the experiences of the first weeks and months would be charged with emotional significance and so more likely to be recalled with a high degree of accuracy and self-awareness. Each woman was interviewed four times, once before enrolment and once in each term of her first year. All the interviews were tape-recorded and subsequently transcribed. From these recordings I learned how they survived initial rites of passage like writing their first essay, holding their own in seminar discussions, coping with teaching practice and revising for end of year examinations. In the middle of the first year the women were also asked to keep a diary for a continuous ten to fourteen day period in which they recorded everything they did from the moment they got up in the morning until the time they went to bed.

I then interviewed a small subgroup of seven women, all then in their third year of teaching, to investigate their experience of job applications, being interviewed and their first year of teaching. In order to preserve the anonymity of the women, members of their families and the teachers with whom they were working, fictitious names have been used throughout.

The educational and political context

The period in which the women underwent their initial training was a time of turbulent change in English education and politics. The impact of the 1988 Education Reform Act had worked its way through schools and higher education institutions and the prescriptions and discourse of the National Curriculum had entered the daily lives of teachers, teacher educators and pupils. Control of education funding was moving away from Local Education Authorities into Local Management of Schools. These women were among the first cohorts of student teachers to be trained to cope fully with all aspects of the Education Reform Act and to see its impact on the resourcing and day-to-day administration of state schools.

The student lives of the women in the study were shaped by sweeping and dramatic changes in education and the political economy. Several became casualties of the economic and social changes which took place during the course of their training as house repossessions, debt and family redundancies were encountered. While these difficulties caused anxiety and some severe personal and familial crises, they resolutely refused to give up on the course. This tenacity and single-minded determination to achieve their ambition to teach in the face of daunting problems impressed me greatly as I listened to the ways in which these events were affecting their lives.

Content of the book

Chapter 1 examines what is special about teaching and why so many teachers continue to find it stimulating. It stresses the importance of ensuring that the timing of the decision to teach is right both for the potential student and the family. The significance of getting into training by taking up some form of preparatory study is emphasised. Advice is given on entry qualifications and how to prepare for the interview. Using diary extracts and the subjective accounts of the women's early student experience, Chapter 2 examines the daily reality of learning how to become a student teacher and offers helpful strategies to ease the 'settling in' process including the early establishment of compatible friendship groups. The mysteries of higher education such as the difference between a lecture, seminar and tutorial, for example, are explained and advice is given on how to take notes, get the most from tutors and how to avoid becoming overwhelmed by the library. Chapter 3 discusses the kind of coping strategies which the women constructed in order to ensure academic success without causing conflict and strained relationships at home. These are not recipe knowledge but differ according to the social, material and biographical circumstances of the individual. Detailed advice on how to tackle the first essay is given along with a survivor's guide to examination revision. The women's first perceptions of teaching practice are the focus of Chapter 4. Anticipated with pleasure and confident expectation, teaching placements do not always match expectations and sometimes result in contradictory and disappointing outcomes. However, fraught and contradictory experiences often lead to positive and rewarding learning, one outcome of which is the gradual emergence of a student teacher identity. In chapter 5 the issue of job applications is taken up along with the question of how student teachers can best sell themselves in their letter of application and job interview. Explicit guidance is given on interview preparation including advice on how to make a presentation and construct a portfolio of teaching evidence, both of which are now becoming a common requirement of teaching applicants. The Chapter also includes a section on how to deal positively with disappointment and with apparent rejection when students do not succeed in achieving the post they applied for. The experience of the first year of teaching is explored in Chapter 6. Defining moments which mark the transition to qualified teacher status are examined with the help of a series of first-hand accounts drawn from the follow-up study. Mentor relationships, job satisfaction and career development are discussed in detail as highly significant features of the first year which can enhance or diminish the novice teacher's sensibilities.

Note

1   Some research attention has been given to the experience of mature women undergoing B.A. and B.Sc courses (see for example, Edwards, 1993 and Pascall, and Cox, 1993). There are also some American studies which have investigated the training and career paths of women lawyers and physicians (see for example, Epstein, 1983 and Lorber, 1984). Surprisingly, there are no studies of mature women student teachers.

Chapter 1

Making the decision to teach

What will I learn from this book?

This book will take you through the significant staging posts on the journey from student to qualified teacher status. Drawing on research on mature women student teachers the book sets out to give you helpful suggestions about how to make the best of your B.Ed course.

By the end of the book you should:

- be clearer about what is involved in a full-time undergraduate course[1] of teacher training

- have gained some guidance about a range of student teacher hurdles including how to write your first essay, cope with your first teaching placement, manage both family and academic responsibilities and prepare for your first job interview

- have learned the value of coping strategies by reading about some of the best and worst moments of the women in the research group who trained in the early 1990s and who are now in their first years of teaching

- have confirmed for yourself that teaching either is or is not really for you

- have become aware that in addition to training you to be a teacher, the course is also likely to change you as an individual.

The book can be read from cover to cover as a continuous whole or dipped into for the parts which interest you most. It can also be used during the course of your training as a source of reference, reassurance and possible inspiration!

If you are in the process of deciding to train for teaching you are unlikely to have reached this point without a great deal of soul searching and careful preparation. Your decision to act and take the next step of applying for a course of teacher training will not, I suspect, have come to you in a sudden moment of truth but rather as a slow and gradual realisation that it is now possible given the particular circumstances of your life and family's needs. You may have wanted to teach since early childhood but, for one reason or another, were denied or forfeited the opportunity. The seeds of your aspiration may not have taken root until you became a mother and a fascinated observer of your children's learning and development. You may have helped at your children's playgroup, toddler group or primary classroom and ended up enjoying and gaining immense satisfaction from helping other children to learn. Perhaps a teacher or playgroup leader encouraged your growing interest in taking up teaching by telling you that you were successful in your work with children and that they valued the part you had played in helping them to make progress. The possibility of becoming a teacher then becomes an ever present thought in your mind finding its way into your everyday conversation with yourself and others.

As you ponder on whether teaching is a real possibility or a pipe-dream which is best forgotten, you ask yourself these questions: Can I manage a full-time course of teacher training as well as run a home and manage the family? Are my school days so far behind me that I will have forgotten how to retain facts from books or write an essay? Will I be able to afford to give up my job in order to become a student teacher, keep up the mortgage payments and buy textbooks? Will it be possible to drop the children off at school and get to lectures on time? If any of these thoughts and questions speak to your experience then this book will be a source of useful information, advice and reassurance to you. In addition, you will be able to draw comfort from the knowledge that other women in your position have been through the same process of self examination, struggled with the same doubts and not only succeeded in surviving the course, but enjoyed it and did well.

What's so special about teaching?

Teaching is hazardous. So, behind and around the teachers, and before and beneath them, is the world of educational administration – the world of planning, time-tabling, resourcing, allocating, checking, budgeting, appointing, employing, building, repairing, lecturing, advising, inspecting. This latter world is the water in which teachers swim, a theatre in which they perform and play, a home in which they can relax and chat, a village or a city in which they exchange and meet, deliberate and wonder, strive and stumble, struggle and succeed.[2]

Teaching is one of the most worthwhile and rewarding professions. But like any career which is high on satisfaction it exacts great energy and effort before the rewards can be reaped and teaching is probably greedier than most on mental, emotional and physical stamina. So the ability to sustain a high level of productive energy on a daily basis over several weeks is an important prerequisite of teaching. Most teachers care enormously about the children they teach and invest a great deal of themselves in the process of helping them learn,[3] whether it be the first faltering steps a five-year old takes in learning to read, or challenging a group of eleven-year olds to write, edit and sell their own school newspaper. When children succeed in making progress in the early stages of learning or in the later, more sophisticated levels of applied knowledge and group collaboration, a teacher has worked towards this end systematically and patiently over many weeks and months. When success of this kind is experienced, it is usually hard won with fits and starts along the way, but it is always deeply gratifying to see children motivated, interested in what they are doing and proud of their accomplishments.

Getting the buzz

Although the rewards do not come easily, the uplift and surge of adrenaline when they do show up are richly rewarding and help to sustain you during the leaner times. I have just received a letter from an ex-primary pupil of mine called Zena, who wrote to tell me that she had successfully completed her undergraduate studies in Italian at Edinburgh University with a 2:1 degree. She is now in her early twenties and has been writing to me for over thirteen years. She was a very able and highly motivated pupil who was a privilege and pleasure to teach and I am not in the least bit surprised about her excellent degree result, but I only taught her for a term, when I was acting head-teacher of a rural primary school, in between posts in higher education. The class she was in was a lively, but understretched group of ten and eleven year olds in their final year of primary school and I had to work hard and fast to bring them up to speed in preparation for their first years of secondary schooling. The class was challenging and demanding but I loved working with them and such was the impact of their vibrant personalities that I can still recall most of them. Now, several years later, Zena bothers to write and tell me her latest news and, most touching of all, she still remembers me as an inspiring teacher. Feeling tired and jaded at the end of a particularly difficult year in higher education, her words have helped to uplift and spur me on in the writing of this book. The point of this personal anecdote is to emphasise the lasting impact which committed teaching can have on pupils, even in a relatively short time. Let there be no mistake, there is a price to pay for this kind of single-minded professional and personal investment in terms of fatigue and loss of space and time. But the 'buzz' teachers get from seeing their pupils do well and from their un-inhibited enthusiasm to work 'out of their skins' when they feel confident and secure in what they're doing, is one of the most frequently mentioned reasons which teachers give for staying in teaching – even when they're facing insuperable difficulties and coping with seemingly endless changes in educational legislation and policy initiatives.

The flip side

You will not be surprised to hear, however, that classroom life is not always so upbeat and rewarding. A great deal of effective teaching is underpinned by the day to day routines of the management of behaviour, planning, assessing and writing reports. The administration now required of teachers is probably more intensive than at any other time and, for some teachers, this part of their job is perceived as arduous, time-consuming and unrewarding. There are also the bleak and bad days when the children are restless, disinclined to work, when parents' complaints are pressing and the day's planning is sabotaged by a trail of interruptions. Nobody escapes these days of 'paradise lost'. The key to an avoidance of despair at such times is to remember the successes and the 'Zenas' of this world and firmly resist the temptation to dwell on what may be one bad day amid several reasonable ones. Teachers do not, of course, have a monopoly on black days; doctors, lawyers, nurses and company directors have them too.

The reality of teaching

The profession needs people who are innovators and problem solvers; who can think on their feet, play as a team, who thrive on challenge and the pressure to meet deadlines; who can see alternative possibilities in situations which appear to be problematic and who like working with people in a bustling atmosphere of noise and constant movement. If you can take the paperwork in your stride, you stand a chance that some deeply satisfying moments of learning will take place somewhere in the complex interactions between you and your class. If any of this gives you a frisson of excitement and challenge, then teaching is for you. The downside is that teaching is not a profession which fits neatly into clearly bounded compartments of time. When the teaching day is over and the children have gone home, there are countless things to do in preparation for the next day in addition to staff meetings, parents' evenings and meetings with school governors. Some of these meetings can stretch well into the evening and the demands of teaching will frequently spill over into your evenings and weekends. The holidays are long and an attractive feature of the job but you need them to recover from the cumulative drain on your energy which interacting with thirty or more children soaks up. In addition, some of the holiday time will be taken up with preparation for the next term, curriculum development plans and writing reports on pupils' progress.

At the time of writing, the salary for a newly qualified teacher with a good honours degree is £15,012.[4] Whilst the salary for beginning teachers has slowly improved in recent years in comparison to other professions, it is still considered by many to be inadequate, given the current responsibilities and sharply increased work load of the job. However, schools can now, at their discretion, pay considerably more than the basic salary to newly qualified teachers, especially if they are able to offer expertise in a shortage subject area. So, some way down the line, when you are making job applications, it may be worth asking whether your starting salary is negotiable, especially if you know that what you have to offer is in short supply at the school. But few teachers are attracted to the profession because of its financial rewards!

Be prepared for the interview

If you have spent some time working in schools as a parent-helper or school governor, you are likely to be aware of some of what it means to be a teacher. If not, the points I have made need serious thought or testing out in a local school with some voluntary work if you have not yet encountered the reality of working with children in a primary classroom. This experience will also provide a focused talking point at an interview in a teacher training institution. It will be helpful if you think in advance about why you want to teach. This question is frequently asked but many student teacher candidates come unprepared for it despite its obviousness to education tutors and school representatives on the interview panel. Try to think beyond your affection and liking for children. Such self evident truisms often fail to impress interview panels. What they are more interested in is your understanding of what it means to work with children in a school context and why this is potentially interesting to you as a career. Apart from the inevitable differences between individuals, your reasons for wanting to teach need to centre on the relationship between children, learning and the myriad complexities which lie within this intensely interesting process. You will feel stronger and more confident if your part in this process and why you want to be involved in it, receives some focused and clear thinking before you make an application for a course of teacher training.

The timing of your decision to teach

At the beginning of this chapter I suggested that you may already have put a great deal of thought behind your decision to teach. Part of your thinking may be centred on whether the time to enter the teaching profession is right for you and your family. This was certainly a preoccupation with the women in the study and the language they used indicated the extent to which it had shaped their thinking: 'the time is right,' 'now is the time,' 'this is the right time for me,' 'if I don't do it now, it will be too late,' 'I'm ready for a change.' When I asked Linda Vince, a thirty-nine year old mother of two boys and a parent-helper at her local school, what had led up to her decision to train for teaching, she replied :

> ... Partly the push from my headmaster that I'd got it in me to do it. A little girl's dream. I wanted to be a missionary in India who taught maths. I want an occupation that's going to leave me spending the rest of my life with children now mine have grown up and I wanted children to fill the gap when mine leave home.

Linda mentions not one but five factors which underpin her decision, each linked to various points in her life history: encouragement and belief in her ability from the headmaster of the school in which she was currently helping as a parent; a vocational desire which goes back to the age of 10 years when mathematics was her favourite subject; a wish to work with children and a need to have something worthwhile to fill her life once her own children had left home or no longer needed her sustained attention. This casting back and forth in her life's history to find a response to my question was a pattern which was repeated by most of the women in the study. Indeed, the question appeared to serve as a trigger to an unfolding narrative in which the women tracked through their lives to find points of transition which related to their decision to teach.

An early finding in my research was that the decision to teach for mature women was not generally the result of a sudden change of heart in which a new career plan emerged with clarity and direction. The aspiration to teach had often surfaced in childhood, faded away at the end of secondary schooling, been temporarily displaced by marriage and a range of work experiences, usually unconnected with teaching, and resurfaced at some point during motherhood. The decision to teach was caught up with a series of interconnecting strands in the women's life histories which appeared to come together with some kind of involvement in classroom life and growing independence on the part of their children which allowed space for self development and potential career fulfilment. Making the decision to teach involved an assessment of their past lives from their perspective as mothers from which they could weigh up the possibility of pursuing a cherished, but so far, un-gratified, career ambition. The point at which the women felt the time was right for them varied between individuals and their understanding of when they believed their families were most able to adjust to the demands that their new roles as full-time students would make upon them. For some of the women this was when their children were about to enter secondary schooling; for others, it was when they were settled either at the infant or junior phase of primary schooling and, for one woman, it was shortly after the birth of her baby. The relationship bet-ween time and age in the women and their families was important in understanding their responses to my question and I return to this theme later in the chapter.

The women in the study

As the journey of the women's progress as student teachers unfolds you may find it helpful to refer to their biographical details in the appendix, pp.133-6. which gives a thumbnail sketch of each of the twenty-five women in the study. In order to preserve the confidentiality of the women, fictitious names have been used throughout.

With the exception of a 24 year old unmarried student of Asian Indian ethnic origin, all the women were white and had between one and three children. One was in a long term relationship with a male partner, one was divorced and the remaining twenty-two were married when I began the study. On the whole, the women referred to their marriage partners as 'husbands' and to themselves as 'wives'.[5] The women were chosen for their broad representation across age, work experience and B.Ed entry route.[6] I tried to obtain a more evenly distributed mix of married and unmarried women with and without children but the mature women applicants during the year of the study were mostly married mothers who therefore became the dominant group in the investigation.

Why no men?

I decided to focus on mature female students for two main reasons: in the early 1990s women formed the large majority of students compared to men on B.Ed courses with females consistently representing 90% of the student population with males seldom representing more than 10% in any one year of the course.[7] Secondly, studies of women in institutions of higher education are relatively rare and, until recently, even less was known about the experiences of mature women in higher education.

This does not mean that men are not worthy of study. Indeed, the fact that they represent such a consistently small minority of students on primary teaching courses may make them a particularly interesting group to research. Since I completed the study, I have addressed conferences in Britain and abroad and, on several occasions, men in the audience have approached me afterwards to say how much they identified with some of the points I had made about the experience of mature women and that a study of their experience as mature males is long overdue. I am broadly in agreement with this view but I would also argue that whilst there may be some common ground in the training experiences of both men and women, the fact that women continue to shoulder the main burden of childcare leads me to conclude that student-teacher mothers have qualitatively different needs and experiences from student-teacher fathers.[8]

The realisation of a dream

> ... it gradually came to me that this sort of dream of primary school teaching ... I don't know why I couldn't do it. Why not?

Pauline Cash, like Linda Vince in an earlier tape recorded extract, expresses her wish to teach as a dream, a dream which had lain unfulfilled for many years. She enjoyed the years of watching her children grow up, but now both are at school. For a few hours in the day the house is empty and she has time to think about what she would like to do in the future. She could return to the office job she had before having children, but she recognises that this would not sustain her interest for very long. It is at this point that the possibility of realising her dream begins to take shape. The fusion of greater periods of time for reflection, increased personal confidence as a result of the experience of motherhood and the re-emergence of the desire to teach, all unite in a firmer resolve to act upon what has up till now been an unrealised dream. It is a significant turning point in a lengthy, reflective process which eventually leads to a firm decision to apply for a course of teacher training.

Getting the timing right

What was striking about the women's responses to my question, 'Why take up teaching now?' was their firm conviction that the moment to act on their decision had arrived. Much of the sure-footedness about the timing of their decision related to three factors: the beginnings of restiveness now that the children no longer needed so much of their time and attention; a realisation that they did not want to return to the job they had prior to motherhood and a desire 'for something more' than the voluntary work in schools many of them were involved in. How all these factors came together is clearly articulated in the following interview extract with Pauline Cash:

DD How far do you feel that your experience in paid employment, your voluntary as a mother helper and life experience as a mother relates to your wish to teach?

PC ... I suppose everything in a way. Everything relates to ... What I've done before, I know I don't want to do again. I mean that's the negative view of it but I want to do more and I feel I'm capable of doing more.

DD So why take up teaching now?

PC Well, I never felt that I wanted to go out to work while the children were young. I've always enjoyed being at home with them. I think once the first one started school, then it made me realise that I'm not going to be happy at home while they're not. I knew I couldn't stand office work for very long. I also know I wanted to learn more as well and improve my academic qualifications and it gradually came to me that this sort of dream of primary school teaching ... that you know ... I don't know why I couldn't do it. Why not?

Between the lines of this extract is a sense that being a mother has changed Pauline. Motherhood has given her another 'lens' to reflect on what she had done in the past and what she might do in the future ...'What I've done before, I know I don't want to do again ... I want to do more ...' Many of the women acknowledged that being a mother had changed them as people and made them look at their lives from a new perspective. In all cases, the changes with respect to enhanced self-esteem and confidence as well as insights gained about their children's development and learning, were viewed positively. Another important point is that whilst the skills and knowledge gained by the women in their roles as mothers and volunteer helpers in school and other organisations do not often count in the labour market,[9] teaching is one of the few professions where these skills are valued and perceived as relevant. Mature women applicants should therefore feel confident about the significance of their life experiences to a career in teaching.[10]

The close relationship between parenting, voluntary work in school and teaching was judged by Beth Wells to have played a strong part in re-energising her wish to teach:

... As a parent I feel I've always been a teacher and my children are doing very well at school and even with other people's children it comes naturally to me. I sort of sit down with them and play with them and read to them. It comes naturally with me that when I'm with children, I sort of take over the teaching role. I can't explain it ... but really it's since having my own children

and since getting so much as a parent-helper. I felt I wanted to do more than
be a helper. I thought I would like the challenge of having a class of my own
and I just feel that I've got a lot to give and I felt that being a parent-helper
was rewarding but I felt I could do more.

Beth explains clearly here how motherhood and teaching are continuous with one another. In addition, the experience of being a parent-helper confirms her teaching ability in the context of the classroom. The work is rewarding and, as a consequence, she realises that she has a lot to give as a helper but it is not enough to satisfy her in the long term. She knows and feels that she 'could do more.' Part of the turning point from which the women felt they could act on their decision to teach arises not only from the meshing together of the life experiences I have outlined, but from a mood state which can loosely be described as a restive searching for a career direction which would give them the challenge and fulfilment they crave.

Beth's mood of aimlessness combined with her two children's transfer to secondary and junior school, convinced her that the time was right, if not overdue, for her to consider becoming a student teacher.

... I feel at the moment sort of aimless. Although I do lots of interesting
things. I do feel sort of aimless and I feel as if I should have applied a year,
perhaps two years ago, because as the children are growing up, they need
me less and less ... I don't know ... I just feel that for me now, the time is
right. My daughter starts secondary school in September and my son starts
junior school at the same time. I don't know ... there's just something inside
me that says the time is right. I just feel that I do not want another year of
doing ... well, similar things. I want something more.

Involve the family

So far I have looked at some of the factors in the complex thought processes involved in the women's decision to teach. I hope that some of the experiences I have recounted will resonate with your thinking and at least confirm for you that others have been through a similar process. If you are at or past the stage of making your decision, you will already have appreciated that getting this part of the staging-post right, is a very important first step. You will also know that it is not simply an individual decision but one which involves a carefully managed negotiation between you and the family. If you look back at the extract with Beth you will see that at one level, the timing of her decision is based on intuition – 'there's just something inside me that says the time is right.' But she has also observed that the children are increasingly less dependent on her and that she wants a change and greater challenge in her life. It does, of course, matter that decisions which will bring about significant changes to your life 'feel right' to you in terms of their timing and long term implications. But once you become a full-time student, domestic routines will change for your family, so if you want your family's support in your new career, it is in your interest to keep them informed and involved in your decision and all that flows from it.

Become an information seeker and get a step ahead

The clearer your family are about the kind of commitment you will be taking on for four years, the better they will be able to support you when you are on the course. For example, some of the women I studied found out before they began the course what kind of hours they would be required to be on campus for taught sessions and when lectures started and finished. It was a surprise and a relief to them to learn that they did not have to travel to the college every day and that on at least one or two days, they were able to work at home. This kind of advance information makes all the difference to women with complex family commitments and childcare arrangements. By reducing the unknown and uncertain in this way, you can bring the course and its demands within your control. So once you have been offered a place on a course, find out from the course leader what the expectations are for the first term with respect to attendance and course assignments. Whilst under-graduate teacher training programmes follow broadly similar patterns, institutions differ in their demands and expectations of students, so the more you know the better you will be able to plan and think ahead about how you can manage the home and keep abreast of academic commitments.

Your family will find it helpful to have this kind of detail so that they know what to expect too. The women in the study who were most at ease with the course and their changing life styles ensured that they kept their families involved and interested in what they were doing. Children particularly appreciated being taken to the campus to see where their mother's 'classrooms' were, and what the computer and library facilities were like, for example. Indeed, some of the children regularly came to the campus library to search for books for school projects or to do their homework. Not only did they enjoy working in the large, adult culture of a college library, but they were learning how to make use of advanced library skills alongside their student mothers which, in turn, would help them in their own development and education. Most children too, at some time or other, experience a student teacher in their classrooms, so their interest in what goes on 'behind the scenes' and how their mothers are being taught is likely to be very high. In addition, the children of the women in the study were often very proud of the fact that their mothers were training to become teachers and were keen to act as 'guinea pigs' for trial lessons to be used on school placements. The women often commented on how useful their own children's responses had been especially with respect to difficulties in the understanding and application of new concepts which they had not anticipated and which might not have come to light until the lesson was underway with a class of twenty-five or more pupils.

Once your family have a clearer picture about what you are going to be doing both on the course and at home it will be easier to enlist their help with the domestic routines. It may seem obvious – but the family's understanding of the part they will need to play in sharing household chores will be a key part of your decision-making process. The women in the study who did not make it explicit to their families at the outset that once they became full-time students, life at home would change and they would need to help with the work load on a daily basis, expended valuable energy exhorting their reluctant husbands and children to adapt to changes they neither wanted nor anticipated.

Entry qualifications

If you have weighed up all these factors and judge that the time is right for you to make an application, you will need to check that you have the necessary entry qualifications to qualify for mature student entry. This may have been one of your first considerations, in which case you will already have covered the ground set out in this section. If you have not yet reached this point you will find the following information a useful digest of the kind of guidance you should receive from the admissions department of your chosen university or college of higher education.

Some of the women in the study had no formal school leaving quali-fications when they first considered teaching and, as a way of spread-ing the load as well as gradually building up their academic confi-dence, spent several years incrementally gathering the necessary O'levels, GCSEs and A levels at night school and part-time study courses. Others had gained them years ago at secondary school and had no need to top up or gain additional, academic qualifications. Most mature applicants fall somewhere between these two positions.

The basic requirements today are five GCSEs or their equivalents, two of which must be English and mathematics, and at least one A level. Institutions differ in the precise requirement they expect of under-graduate primary teaching applicants but, because of the increased importance of science in the primary National Curriculum, many now insist on a GCSE science or its equivalent, even though it is mandatory only for those applicants born after 1979. Whilst mature students can enter with one rather than two A levels, increasingly subjects are pre-ferred which have a relevance to the National Curriculum, like history, English or geography. Because of the way the National Curriculum now drives most courses of teacher training, you may find that some institutions will no longer accept A levels in General Studies or Com-munication Studies as an entry qualification. Again, it is up to the admitting institution as to what is counted as an acceptable A level alternative and you are advised to consult the undergraduate primary teaching admissions tutor or course leader, for precise mature entry information.

Access courses

An approved and increasingly widely-used route for entry into higher education and B.Ed and BA QTS courses,[11] are locally administered Access courses. These courses are specifically designed to prepare mature students without formal qualifications to enter higher educa-tion. Many local colleges of adult and further education now offer one or two-year part time, Access courses for intending student teachers which include study in the required competencies in English, mathe-matics and science. Part of the course also includes study at an academic level suitable for entry into higher education. Many mature students appreciate the sympathetic guidance and help which are given on these courses, one aim of which is to boost the confidence of students who may not have engaged in formal study since they were last at school. Another attractive feature of these courses is that they provide a package which covers all the necessary entry requirements for teacher training under one roof, thus avoiding the logistical difficulties of 'chasing' the required qualifications in more than one institution.

Subject specialism

Another recent requirement instituted by the Teacher Training Agency[12] is for all student teachers to reach specific standards in subject knowledge, especially in the core subjects of mathematics, English and science. In addition, all students have to acquire at least one subject specialism in which they have sufficient confidence, knowledge and understanding to become future school curriculum leaders or co-ordinators. You will need to decide which subject you wish to specialise in before making your application. It is to your advantage to choose a subject in which you already have some expertise and enthusiasm. Depending on the demand for places (within the chosen subject), institutions may ask for a particular grade at A level. For example, because English is often a popular choice with student teachers, you may find that a higher grade is demanded. Mature students without A levels need not feel disadvantaged by this requirement but you will need to demonstrate at interview that you are sufficiently committed to and interested in the subject to keep abreast of the reading and course assignments. Some catching up with reading and specific subject knowledge may be necessary before you are admitted to the subject specialism programme. Students often welcome the opportunity to take their subject knowledge to a higher level of intellectual challenge and enjoy not only the academic demands of subject study but also the chance to teach a subject they understand in depth.

School experience, personal qualities and the interview

Most universities and colleges offering teacher training courses stipulate that candidates should have at least two to three weeks of continuous classroom experience before being offered a place. This can take the form of voluntary school help, work experience or paid work as a classroom or special needs assistant. This helps both you and the institution confirm that primary teaching is a realistic career option for you. It also provides you with concrete experience of working along-side teachers and children from which you will be able to call up examples of effective and ineffective classroom practice. It is worth thinking in advance about examples of interesting or problematic teaching and learning scenarios which you have observed during an experience of this kind, so that you can retrieve them from memory with ease when you are under pressure to think quickly at an interview.

Another purpose of the interview is to assess whether or not you have the personal qualities to succeed in teaching. You will be asked, for example, to demonstrate that you can communicate clearly, effectively and accurately; to show an ability to listen and take account of the views of others and to give evidence that you are aware of some contemporary issues in education. If you want to be reasonably well informed about the state of play in education, it is a good idea to get into the habit of reading some of the key articles in the educational press like the *Times Educational Supplement* and the education pages of the *Guardian* and *The Independent*, for example. Burning issues in education wax and wane like the moon and no sooner has one 'hot' educational issue hit the headlines when another almost immediately takes its place. It is difficult for even the most assiduous educational news reader to keep on top of the countless new initiatives which are sweeping our classrooms in waves of change. So do not expect to know all there is to know in education before you begin the course. As I write this book, the 'hot stuff' of the moment is the Literacy Hour and the forthcoming Numeracy Hour in September 1999, as well as homework for all primary children. There is currently no shortage of lineage on these subjects in the education press and it would help you to present yourself as an informed and aware teaching candidate if you were to update yourself with at least a rudimentary grasp of their main advantages and disadvantages.

Getting into gear: trial runs and rehearsals

The experience of taking an A' level or Access course or similar form of pre-entry study, can prove to be an invaluable testing of the water both for you and your family. Not only will it help you to get into gear for your course of teacher training but it will help you to experience, in a tangible way, what full-time study means in relation to changes in your life style. It will be reassuring to you to know that you can absorb new ideas, cope with complex reading and meet deadlines for assessment. Giving yourself a trial run of this kind will help to reduce any anxiety you may have about taking on a degree course several years after formal schooling. It will also give you some idea of when your study can best be fitted into your domestic routine and where you work most productively. The latter point may appear trivial, but knowing that you work better in the bedroom or alongside the children at the kitchen table, will not only make you feel calmer at the start of the course but will have established a pattern of study which the children and your husband or partner will already have begun to respect. If study facilities like desk space and the computer have to be shared with the family, it is useful to have worked out some kind of rota system which works with the minimum of conflict, beforehand.

Several of the women in the study acknowledged the value of this 'rehearsal' for study as a way of easing them in gently to working habits and practices which stood them in good stead when the pressure of the degree course began to build up.

Linda Vince, for instance, saw her A level and voluntary work as a parent-helper as a 'trial period' which gave both herself and her family a chance to see whether her commitments outside the home could be successfully integrated into family life.

> ... we've had like a two-year trial period where I've actually been going out every day and sometimes I've had to go in the holidays when they're at home. Gradually we've given the oldest one a bit more responsibility. He's coming up fourteen now and I can trust him completely but I still get the little one looked after. I still feel he needs a home base. I've been out five days a week this year and it will be four days a week for the coming year. I've done an A level course with the 16 year olds at a local school.

Given the priority Linda attached to her responsibilities as a mother, she needed to minimise potential dislocation in her family life. So she carefully orchestrated the changes in her life in an incremental, step-at-a-time approach from which she did not move forward until she was confident that her family was adjusting and adapting to the changes. Only by adopting a cautious, trial and error approach did Linda feel she could move forward to become a teacher. She needed and wanted to take the family with her so that her future years as a full-time student would become an inextricable part of her family life from which they all stood to gain. This process was already underway before she started her teacher training course and, as she explains in the following extract, her A level study resulted in a series of two-way advantages:

DD So both you and the family have had a taster of what life will be like when you become a full-time student?

LV Yes and I think it's done us all good. It's made the children realise that Mum's got this to do and that to do and it's made them help out a little bit, not a lot, but they do a little. It's helped the oldest one a lot because he sees Mum doing homework whilst he's sitting doing his. There's been a lot of discussion about who's doing what. The A level study has brought me up to date and I can now help my children which to me is wonderful.

Women sometimes believe that taking up a career whilst simultaneously bringing up a family is a selfish act and even when they don't take this view themselves, there is always the possibility that others might. An important but often overlooked issue is that when women in Linda's position decide to take an action with respect to their own potential career development, the children learn that their mother has needs and wishes – no bad thing for a growing child to recognise.. Linda's children had also begun to help in the home, albeit in a limited way, and her study alongside them provided a positive role model. Parellel with her mothering role, new knowledge gained during the A level study has also enabled her to help with her children's homework.

An equally important consequence of study rehearsals is the heightened sense of achievement and increase in self-esteem and academic confidence which they can bring. The enjoyment and success Linda experienced on her A level course made her feel that she was '... suddenly an independent woman and not the little woman at the sink any more.' The re-discovery, through study, of self and identity beyond that of mothering and domesticity, can be energising and liberating. Pamela Jones described the euphoria which she felt when she experienced success as an Open University student prior to enrolling on a B.Ed course:

PJ   I'm not somebody's mother and somebody's wife anymore, I'm a person in my own right. It's as simple as that. I feel as though I've got some worth. It's lovely. I've got a first name again.

DD That really matters to you?

PJ   Definitely. My husband knew when he married me that he wasn't going to marry somebody he could keep barefoot and pregnant. He wouldn't even have tried! I'm having a second life. I really feel as though I'm having a second life. I've got a second chance and I'm going to make the most of it.

However, the transition from a predominantly domestic role or from another career to a student role, is not without its difficulties along the way. Part of the problem inherent in any change for women with multiple roles is the temptation to go for the top in all of them – the perfectionist syndrome! What happens then is that every nerve, fibre and muscle is stretched to maximum capacity and, in the end, something gives way. This was what happened to Linda, although fortunately for her, it was during her 'trial period' so she was able to do something constructive to pull back from mission impossible before starting the B.Ed course. The following account shows how Linda succeeded in reaching a workable compromise by negotiation with the family:

LV When I started, I tried to be the perfect mother, the perfect wife, the perfect student – and you can't do it.

DD So what changes did you make?

LV I still kept everything as a student but I tried to reorganise slightly so that I had a little bit of space at home. So I delegated here (at home). We were very much a family where I was the homemaker and Tom was the provider. I did the garden and Tom did the allotment. And we had a team talk and the children did their bedrooms and Tom would hoover through for me if he was on shift at home. We just worked together. We'd all had very independent roles until then and everything to do with the home was mine and I just found I couldn't cope. I think I also stopped expecting myself to be superwoman because I went in with the attitude that my husband's and my children's lives were not going to be affected by something I wanted to do. Their lives *have* been affected but I think they've gained from it.

What Linda had learned at an early point was that adaptations and adjustments to new patterns and routines have to be made at the first sign of crisis. Battling on in order to maintain the status quo may help to get you through the early struggles but in the longer term, this strategy is likely to lead to an intolerable strain for you and the family. It was a significant learning point for Linda to realise that she could not prevent her family's lives from being affected by her wish to study and train for teaching. So she stopped trying to cushion them by reducing the demands she was making on herself and persuaded them to make changes *with* her, believing that they would gain rather than lose from the deal.

Several of the women in my study did not reach this point of under-standing with themselves and their families until they were well launched on the course. In the end, this may not have made a measurable difference to their success and enjoyment on the course, but I have quoted Linda's experiences at length because they clearly demonstrate the value of ironing out some of the difficulties of becoming a student during a trial run when the stakes and pressures are not quite so high.

Many of you will have had or are currently engaged in your own rehearsal before becoming a full-time student and your experience may be quite different from Linda's. What matters is that you have begun to find out what works and what doesn't work with respect to your study routines. The family will have begun to get used to seeing you sitting at a desk or table working with your books and notes for several hours each week. There may have been irritating problems on the way which by now you have either sorted out or are in the process of doing so. If you have not got this far, then at least you now have identified those issues which will need to be resolved at an early point once you're underway as a student teacher. It is worth remembering too, that in a sense, much of your life as a mother has been a kind of rehearsal for thinking about and observing the way in which children learn. Similarly, if you have spent time working in schools as a paid or volun-teer helper you will have an insider's knowledge of what teaching is about which will prove to be an invaluable source of data against which to make sense of theoretical concepts and professional principles as well as your own development as a noviciate teacher.

If you are not currently taking a course of study in preparation for entry onto a teacher training course, it will help you to tune into some impor-tant and interesting educational matters if you get into the habit of making a note of educational programmes on the television and radio and recording them so that you can watch or listen to them when you can give them your full attention. Better still, if you can find an interested friend to watch them with you and discuss them afterwards, you will have begun to practise the skill of questioning debate which will form an important part of your training. If this is not possible, make a note of those issues which puzzled you or which you found particularly interesting and follow them up with further reading in your local library. The Open University Learning Zone also offers some excellent programmes on education and child development which are well worth following but, because of their after-midnight scheduling, most people record them for later viewing.

The final section of this chapter has suggested a number of ways in which you can get into gear with your mind well tuned to the start of your course. The next chapter will take you into the first days and weeks of what it feels like to be a student teacher.

Notes

1   My research on mature women student focused on the training process of a four-year B.Ed course. The experiences of mature women on three-year BA QTS or one-year PGCE courses may be significantly different.

2   Taken from Richardson, R. (1990) *Daring to be a Teacher*. Stoke on Trent: Trentham Books Ltd., p.3. An inspiring and uplifting book for anyone interested in becoming a teacher.

3   For an interesting discussion about the extent to which teachers invest themselves in their work, see Nias, J. (1989) *Primary Teachers Talking: A study of Teaching As Work*. London: Routledge.

4   The basic salary of £15,012 applies with effect from December 1st, 1998 and is part of a recently negotiated phased pay award.

5   To avoid the inelegant use of 'husband/partner' throughout the book as well as the possibility of offending the women, I have used the same titles that the women themselves used when speaking about their marriage and their domestic responsibilities. The label, 'partner' is only used when referring to the one woman to whom this nomenclature applied.

6   The term 'B.Ed entry route' refers to the particular qualifying pathway the women had chosen in order to gain admittance under the mature student entry regulations of the training course. Examples of these were: A' levels gained recently or some years ago whilst at secondary school; local Access courses; Open University Foundation Courses; BTEC (British Technical and Education Council) diplomas

or certificates, etc. A number of the women who already possessed the required entry qualifications enrolled on Fresh Start or Return to Study courses in order to update their study skills. Several of the women in the research group had achieved qualifications well in excess of the entry requirements.

7   A similar picture is reported for 1998. According to 1998 UCAS (Universities and Colleges Admissions Service) statistics, the ratio of female to male for all ages of primary teaching is 89.1% to 10.9%.

8   The exception to this would be the case of male student fathers who were the sole carers of their children. With rising divorce rates and the slight, but growing incidence of lone parent fathers, this is an area urgently in need of research attention.

9   For a more detailed discussion of this point, see Bird, E. and West, J. (1987) 'Interrupted Lives: A Study of Women Returners', in Allatt, P. et al., (Eds) *Women and the Life Cycle: Transitions and Turning-Points,* Basingstoke: Macmillan: pp. 178-91.

10 A note of caution is sounded here. Whilst the teaching profession and HE institutions have, on the whole, valued the contribution that mature women can bring to schools and teacher training courses, examples of covert resistance towards mothers with dependent children, can occasionally be found in educational institutions. There may also be negative career implications for women who bind connections between motherhood and teaching too tightly. H.Burgess, for example, argues that 'a strongly held allegiance to the notion of 'mother in the classroom', may unknowingly support the career trap which prevents many very able women teachers from applying for promotion ...' (1989, p.86).

11 The four-year B.Ed course is not the only undergraduate route to qualified teacher status. A number of institutions now offer 3 year B.Ed and BA QTS courses. An advantage of the latter route is that if a student decides, part way through the course, that teaching is no longer a suitable career option then s/he may elect to continue on the course but end up with a degree in education without qualified teacher status.

12 The Teacher Training Agency (TTA) is a quango set up in September 1994 by the Conservative Government with the purpose of making decisions about the curriculum of teacher training courses, funding approved courses and monitoring standards in Initial Teacher Education and Continuing Professional Development courses.

Chapter 2

The first weeks

Do it your way

During your first encounters as a student teacher you can expect to feel as though you are on an emotional roller coaster. You will feel exhilarated, enthused, disappointed, capable, inadequate, overwhelmed and exhausted, almost on a daily basis. This is a normal reaction to what a professor of psychology once explained to me was 'structured anxiety', a necessary feature of any new undertaking where significant change and increased intellectual expectations are required in order to achieve a desired goal. Nagging doubts that you are not 'up to it', that you may have made a mistake in coming on the course or that there is too much for your brain to take in, are common to most people's experience at some point at the start of a new venture. Some days you will feel on top of the ideas and new knowledge being presented to you; on others, you will feel out of your depth. The sense of struggle and discomfort which you will feel in the early days is an inevitable part of an adjustment to new routines and expectations which will eventually become more predictable, familiar and manageable.

Whatever reaction you have as beginning student teachers, and it will differ depending on the individual and the institution you are attending, it is important that you see yourselves as creative individuals and seekers of solutions[1] who have some degree of control over the changes which will affect you as you learn to become student teachers. Central to this perception of yourselves is what Lortie (1975), in his classical study of American schoolteachers, referred to as the 'self-socialisation' of teachers in which, 'one's personal predispositions are not only relevant but, in fact, stand at the core of becoming a teacher' (p.79). What this means is that you are capable of intervening and shaping your own processes of change in student teacher adaptation according to your own particular needs and interests, a key part of which will include your reality as a mother and wife or partner. So, however overwhelmed and burdened you feel by the vast array of new vocabulary, skills, routines, new ways of seeing and understanding familiar problems, you need to hold onto the view that you are not a helpless, passive recipient who has to accept everything in the way it is presented to you. You will find your own way of adjusting to new practices and accommodating to new concepts and ways of working. There is no preferred method or magic formula for effective study; you have to experiment with place, method and time until you discover what works for you, allow it to become a habit and then stick to it.

The first day

Watch out for the traffic on the first day! In addition to the normal, morning rush hour, you will find that traffic queues are longer than usual, with thousands of students making their way to the local university or college to register for their course. If you have to meet a 9 am deadline for an introductory talk you don't want to add to first-day nerves by arriving late, so allow plenty of time for slow moving traffic, competing for a parking space when you arrive and finding the campus building where your first meeting takes place.

I asked the women in my study to keep a diary of their experiences for the first ten days which included their reactions to what they perceived as 'good' and 'bad' moments. For several women, the first day was blighted by their late arrival into the lecture theatre as a result of unprecedented traffic jams on all the major trunk roads leading to the college. Lucy Patron's diary account of this inauspicious beginning gives some idea of the range of emotions she experienced in the first few hours – excitement, panic, disappointment and frustration:

LP   8.30am. Leaving home. Really excited and anticipating the day. 9.15am. Sheer panic! I'm stuck in traffic and I'm supposed to be here at 9. 0' clock! 1.30pm. We're told to go home again and I felt, oh dear, is that it? Really disappointed and fed up. The next day we spent wandering around and not doing a lot and I really did think, why am I bothering? I think I'll stay at home tomorrow and not come again.

Feeling let down and flat in the first week after so much hard work to get on the course was a cause of initial frustration for many women in the study. They had expected to be immediately engaged in a full programme of activities which was relevant to teaching. That they did very little but complete forms for half a day, came as a surprise and disappointment. Many of them had come straight from the world of work and had been used to the discipline of what they called a 'Nine till five day.' They had geared themselves up for a solid day's work and found that much of it was spent trying to crack the code of complex timetables and finding their way round a large and unfamiliar campus. Being eased in was not what they wanted or expected even though it may well have suited the younger students who had come straight from school and whose main priority was to make friends and sustain sufficient stamina to keep abreast of the endless round of disco parties which are a feature of most fresher weeks.

For Helen Cornwall, this apparent lack of structure and purpose during the first week came as an anti-climax which was compounded by paradoxical feelings of exhaustion as a result of doing what she described as, 'nothing':

HC I'm not going to forget how I felt on that first day because it all came as a bit of an anti-climax, the whole first week. I think I was so excited about coming and when I walked into the lecture theatre on that first morning I didn't feel as nervous as I should do. I looked around and I was surprised at just how many mature students there were. Then I just wanted to get going and I found that first week such hard going. I was shattered by the end of it and I felt shattered through doing nothing.

Whilst this extract is an accurate account of Helen's perception of the first few days, the reality was not quite as bad as it reads. Doing 'nothing' did not, of course, literally mean total inactivity. The women were in a state of highly charged tension in which they were actively engaged in the process of getting to know other students, listening to what course leaders and education tutors were telling them and trying to learn the geography of a large campus. They were, in fact, absorbing immense amounts of new and incoming data about the place in which they were going to spend the next four years. They were trying to read and digest vast quantities of literature connected with course and timetable information in a language and terminology which would have been unfamiliar to them. Lists of books suggested for reading, questions for seminar activities and titles of forthcoming essays were read with a certain amount of awe and dread. They were like strangers in a new and foreign land whose terrain and language they did not understand. They were, for the time being, outsiders in a 'country' they had longed to travel to. But now that they had arrived, it was not as they had hoped.

The first week

Will your experience be the same as this? It is hard to judge because institutions vary considerably in the way they introduce students to their first weeks of teacher training. However, because the tightly packed content of most training programmes is dominated by the primary National Curriculum and the need for specific standards in specialist subject knowledge, many universities and colleges now start formal teaching programmes in the first week, and sometimes on the first day. At least a part of your first day will be taken up with registration, course administration and introductory talks. It will also, at some point, include an induction programme in the use of the library, computer facilities and specialist facilities like literacy centres or mathematics workshops. These sessions are normally organised on a rotating group basis which is spread throughout the first week. Regardless of which practice the institution chooses to adopt, you will almost certainly find that a predictable pattern of timetabled teaching will not normally begin until the second week. Initially, you should expect some time to be taken up with course administration and what may seem endless introductions to tutors and to one another. Wherever you are in higher education, you will not avoid being on the receiving end of a great deal of new information and vast quantities of documentation detailing course programmes, timetables, school placements and the National Curriculum. At times you will feel overburdened and swamped as every new tutor you meet hands out yet another pile of paperwork. Do not be surprised therefore if you feel exhausted in these early days. It is because your brain is having to assimilate and absorb an immense amount of new data, much of it educational jargon which you will soon learn to decode. In order to mitigate the feelings of frustration, incompetence and mental indigestion, the following guidance may help to ease the discomfort of the first few days.

- Expect to feel like a traveller in a strange and unfamiliar land. It will pass as each new day builds on the previous one and some patterns begin to be repeated.

- Take each day as it comes and don't expect to understand everything you are told or are given on paper. You won't and neither will anyone else. When you read your notes and your handouts later, some of it will begin to fall into place and make sense.

- Get into the habit of highlighting or underlining vocabulary, issues and concepts you are not clear about. Give yourself a week or so to try and sort them out and, if they're still bugging you by the end of a week, ask a tutor or talk about it with a friend.

- Make time to have coffee with other students in your group. Talk about how you are feeling and listen to how others are experiencing their first days as student teachers; it helps to know that others are enjoying or finding difficulties with the same things as you.

- Collaboration with and friendship with a group of students can be an invaluable source of inspiration and support. If you dash off on your own or go home immediately a session finishes, you could miss out on key opportunities for group membership. The mature students in my study spoke frequently of how much they appreciated the help and support of friends when crises occurred or when they were feeling low.

- You will be at the receiving end of considerable quantities of paper throughout your training but the initial weighty mass of paper will ease off as the weeks go by. In order to avoid an ever increasing and random pile of unread paperwork cluttering up your desk, you will find it helpful to have a system for organising it so that you can find what you need quickly, from day one. One of the simplest methods is to open up a separate file for each of your taught programmes, for example, English, geography, mathematics etc., and store the relevant paperwork in the appropriate file. You will also need other files for teaching practice information, general professional study courses, course assignments and so on. These can later be divided into sub-sections for further categories within the subject headings. This system is greedy on files but it works. Knowing that you can retrieve what you want when you want it also has the advantage of making you feel that you have some degree of control over your learning.

Settling in

The frantic pace and uncertainty of the first few days will begin to shake down into a regular pattern of timetabled taught sessions by the end of the first or second week. At this point you should find that you are enjoying the lectures and seminar activities, mostly because you will feel that you are now on course with the real business of learning to become a teacher. The women in my research found that these first moments of engagement and absorption with theoretical ideas associated with children's learning were accompanied by physical and psychological feelings of relief and a calmer mental disposition, mostly because they could relate to the material from their lived experience. For example, Anne Major's reaction to the first timetabled session of the term was typical of many of the mature women's accounts of this experience:

AM But on the Friday we had our first proper teaching session and after that, I really felt uplifted. I felt good and I went home for the weekend thinking, 'Oh great! This is good.' It sort of changed from Thursday night to Friday morning and it's done that quite a lot over the first few weeks. It was up and down quite a lot. It was, 'Oh how am I ever going to manage this?' And then at other times, it would be, 'Well, I've done that. I did that alright, you know, it was ok. I can do it.'

The feeling of elation which often accompanied these early teaching sessions was a common experience among the women and it is not difficult to see why. They had undergone arduous preparation with respect to study and family arrangements before they could commit themselves to a full-time course of training. A great deal of self-investment had therefore been expended prior to their enrolment on the course. If they did not succeed or the course did not match their expectations, then a great deal of self-investment would have been wasted and the consequent disruption to their personal and family lives not worth the energy and effort directed into it. Seen from this perspective, it is easy to understand the women's elation when there was a congruence between anticipation and reality, and their feelings of disappointment and despair when they did not feel they could cope with the course or that what they were doing was irrelevant to their purpose. Feeling 'high' and then 'low' would seem to be an inescapable part of the settling in process for mature students.

What actually took place in these first teaching sessions was very important to the women in helping them to adjust to their new role as students. For example, listening to lectures, taking part in seminars, working in the library and taking books home to read for a specific purpose gave them a tangible feeling of engagement with what they considered to be legitimate student activity. But the form and content of the seminar or lecture as well as the teaching style of the tutor, were equally important in enabling them to feel, as one mature student put it, 'that things were beginning to drop into place.' Beth Wells recounted the pleasure she experienced at finding that she could concentrate and absorb the academic content of seminar sessions:

DD So, at what point did you feel that things had started as far as you were concerned?

BW Very early on when we went into groups and started looking at texts and things and certainly by the end of the first week. I surprised myself with my concentration. I feel as if I really am absorbed in what people are giving me all the time and I so look forward to each lecture and I actually lap it up.

Another factor which helped things 'begin to fall into place', was the perceived relevance of the course content with their own experience. Two programmes, for example, were concerned with child development and the development of language from babyhood onwards. These were particularly enjoyed by the women because they were able to relate the conceptual content to their experience of motherhood. Gail Prince makes this point very well in the following extract:

GP ... and you start thinking, oh yes, that makes sense, particularly the Language Development programme in relation to how children learn at home. I was beginning to relate to some of the things on reading which I used to think as a parent, and it sort of eased me into it, if you like. It was coming at it from a different angle ... You start thinking, oh I remember that, and, oh yes, that's why ... you know, and that has begun to fall into place as well.

A further indication of early adjustment was a sense that they were now more in control of events. This was often articulated as 'coping'. Typical expressions were, 'Ok, I'm coping.' 'I can cope with this.' What this meant was that they were beginning to experiment with routines and arrangements which helped them feel they were keeping 'on top of' the many demands that were being made of them. This perception was often accompanied by a discernible release of tension after a strenuous or difficult task had been successfully undertaken. It served as a benchmark of early adaptation which confirmed their belief that they had made the right decision to train as teachers. Up until this point in those early weeks, doubts rather than belief in their ability to make the grade as student teachers, had been uppermost in their minds. Pat Grade articulated the way in which she experienced this moment of transition as one in which she no longer felt 'an outsider':

PG With the Language Development programme, I could understand what was going on. I could contribute. I knew what was happening. Because I did A' level psychology, I could slip in lovely there and I thought, 'Oh well, it's not as bad as I thought it would be.' I could feel the relief flooding into me and I thought, 'Ah, I can relax!' I knew what was being discussed and I didn't feel an outsider ... Now I feel I can cope.

Only the previous week Pat had recorded the following, rueful comment in her diary:

Now more than ever, wished I'd chosen to stay at home or work full-time in Tesco's!

Pat's swing from 'low to high' in just a few days shows just how volatile your emotions are when you are trying to adjust to an important, new experience in your life. This anecdote also succinctly demonstrates how quickly things can change and the commensurate importance of staying cool and holding on when you feel that nothing is as you had hoped and that you are not coping. Such feelings are usually temporary and often quickly displaced by more positive and stable emotions. The other important point to bear in mind is that it is in the institution's interest to keep you motivated on the course through to the point of successful completion. Every student who withdraws from the course results in a subsequent loss of funding from the Teacher Training Agency. But more importantly, most education tutors are very keen to ensure that you find course programmes interesting and stimulating. Many have been successful primary teachers who know from experience that there are few more miserable experiences than a class of children or students who are bored or uninterested in the material you are presenting. Considerable effort therefore goes into the planning stage to make sure that teaching content is accessible, up to date and above all, relevant and engaging. You will recall what I wrote earlier about the importance of the 'buzz' in teaching in helping to sustain high quality teaching and motivation in schools. The same applies to tutors involved in teacher training. Seldom is anything more uplifting and heartening than when a group of students leave a lecture room manifestly enthused about a teaching idea they have just had demonstrated to them. Even more rewarding is when a student returns from a teaching practice and tells their tutor: 'I used that idea you showed us on the course and the children loved it. They got so interested that some of them stayed in at playtime and took the work home to finish.' This is the buzz which sustains and exhilarates education tutors and such is its value and reward in terms of personal and professional satisfaction, that they go to enormous lengths to plan training sessions which maximise student interest and motivation. If students feel good about what they see and hear in the seminar or lecture theatre, because it makes sense to them and can be used to inform a written assignment or stored for later implementation in the classroom, then this gives positive feedback to the tutor. Most education tutors are therefore highly motivated to deliver lectures and seminars which students perceive as interesting, informative and useful.

Lectures, seminars and tutorials: what are they?

You will meet a number of teaching approaches in your course of teacher training. The teaching method used will depend partly upon the subject being taught so that for example, a subject like art or physical education is more likely to have more practical workshops than say, a subject like English which will usually involve a mix of lectures, seminars and practical workshops. This is because the teaching of art is best taught by activity, experimentation and individual involvement with a variety of media, whereas the teaching of English requires all student teachers to possess a common baseline of knowledge and understanding about how to teach reading, or plan for progression in children's writing, for example, which is best done in a well structured lecture. The variety of methods of teaching is also designed to give you a repertoire of approaches which can be applied to the primary classroom. In addition, the demonstration of how to set up, start, develop and conclude these forms of teaching organisation, should serve as a model of exemplary practice which you can emulate and develop on teaching practice.

The lecture

The lecture is an economic and efficient way of imparting specific information or a body of knowledge which is deemed necessary for all students. It is normally delivered to a large group (usually a year group) of students, by one tutor. It will present the key debates, main research findings, contemporary issues and practices of say, the management of behaviour in the classroom. It will often be underpinned by theoretical concepts, educational principles, learning theories and the works of major writers: influential thinkers or practitioners in the field will be referred to and discussed. This form of delivery is often accompanied by overhead transparencies, video material and/or reproduced lecture notes which will include the main outline of the lecture and a list of relevant books, articles and reports, some of which you will be encouraged to read in order to further your understanding.

Your main role will be to listen and take notes. Sometimes you will be invited to raise questions and points of discussion with the lecturer and/or with a nearby group of students. A well crafted, interestingly delivered and skilfully paced lecture can be a very stimulating and valuable learning experience. However, in order to get the best from a lecture, you need to be an efficient note-taker and to have done some preparatory reading so that you are tuned in to some of the important issues and theoretical concepts. The issue of note-taking will be taken up later on in the chapter.

The seminar

In teacher education,[2] a seminar can take two main forms: the first usually follows on from a lecture in which the main ideas are explored, questioned and analysed in order to reach a deeper level of under-standing through shared discussion; the second takes the form of a practical session, sometimes known as a workshop, in which students engage with materials or texts in a specific activity. Using mathe-matical apparatus to show how the concept of subtraction might be taught to a class of children or trying out a piece of computer software to assess its effectiveness in teaching a particular skill, are examples of the practical workshop type of seminar. In practice seminars frequently include a mixture of both these forms. They usually involve smaller groups of roughly fifteen to thirty students, depending on the size of the year group.

In teacher training the preferred age phase for teaching is one of the criteria used for allocating you to a particular seminar group so that you receive training and workshop activities which are appropriate to nursery, Key Stage One (5-7 years) or Key Stage Two (7-11 years), pupils. A seminar tutor is assigned to each group and you will work frequently in these groups giving you an opportunity to build up on-going relationships with both student peers and your tutor. Students generally find the learning which takes place in seminars is crucial for clarifying ideas, understanding the meaning of new terminology and making the connections between theory and application, through discussion and practical activity. Opportunities for raising questions and points of ambiguity with the tutor and fellow students are frequently felt by students to be less intimidating than in the formal lecture context. Central to the learning and enjoyment of these sessions is your involvement and active participation. It is not difficult to take part because seminars are planned to allow maximum group participation through gradual involvement. So if you are not used to speaking in front of a class of students you will find plenty of opportunities to build up your confidence and share your thoughts and reactions firstly with a partner, then a group of four students and so on, before you are expected to speak in front of large group. As you gain confidence during the course, you will be expected to give presentations on specific aspects of teaching to the whole seminar group. So there will be times when the agenda of the seminar is constructed and led by the tutor and others, when it is led and organised by students.

However, in the experience of most tutors, mature students are often among the least likely groups of students to need prompting to lead or take part in discussions. Their life experience and contact with children and classrooms make them more assured in verbal contributions and they usually play a prominent role in seminar activities.

The tutorial

The tutorial provides for a quite different learning opportunity in which you should normally take the lead in bringing specific questions or matters which you wish to discuss with the tutor. These provide for the most personal form of teaching since they usually involve one-to-one contact with a tutor. Typically, tutorials are used for ensuring that students are heading in the right direction with an essay assignment or dissertation. In such circumstances, a student might bring an essay plan, a list of reading with some key points and questions to raise with the tutor for checking and clarification, before writing the essay. In the case of extended essays or dissertations there may be several tutorials before you and your tutor agree that you are ready to write and submit. Again, you are likely to get more out of the tutorial if you come to it prepared with a focused agenda.

In most institutions, students are allocated a tutor who is their personal or academic tutor for the duration of the course. The point of this is to provide you with a named tutor with whom you can request a tutorial if there are personal or academic matters which you wish to discuss privately with someone who has an interest in your overall progress and academic development. This tutor is also likely to be responsible for writing your reference in your final year so it is in your interest to keep her/him in touch with your development over the course.

Individual tutorials will also take place with the tutor responsible for supervising your teaching placement.The purpose of these tutorials is to check and ensure that you have the necessary planning in place to make a secure start on your school practice. Supervising tutors will want to ensure that what you have planned is appropriate and workable for the age group and ability level of the children in your class. They will be able to help you to sharpen your planning where things are not clear and guide your longer term planning. However, the main initiatives and questions should ideally, come from you and not the tutor.

These are the main forms of teaching which you will experience in higher education. The other, significant learning will take place off campus in your various school placements. For many students, sustained contact with children in the classroom where they are taking increasing responsibility for the planning and organisation of lessons, is the point where the various component parts of their training begin to come together and make sense. In addition to these teaching experiences you will be expected to undertake a considerable amount of self directed learning where you will be required to read, undertake specific specific tasks or projects which you might work at on your own or with a group of students.

Getting the best from your tutors

You will have gathered from what I have written earlier that most education tutors are in the business of training students because they enjoy teaching, have been successful practitioners in the classroom, have normally held posts of responsibility and leadership in schools or within a Local Education Authority advisory or inspection service, believe in their subject and teach it well. They want, above all, to pass on their knowledge and enthusiasm to you so that you will, in turn, pass it on to children. You should therefore encounter some very able and experienced education tutors from whom to learn the craft of teaching. Posts in teacher education are highly competitive these days; not only must candidates have the experience and qualities which I have already outlined, but they also have to possess a higher degree and a research publication track record, or at least the potential for developing one. This means that many of the tutors who will be teaching you will also be able to keep you up to date with the latest research findings and much of what they teach you will be enriched by their own research in the subject. Some of the tutors I am currently working with are nationally known figures in their respective research areas and this inevitably brings a sharper edge to their work which energises their teaching.

The work of an education tutor ranges across teaching, research publication and administrative duties. Their teaching also frequently goes beyond undergraduate work and extends to higher degree teaching and thesis supervision as well as running courses for teachers in the evenings. The implications of this are that you may find that when you want to see a tutor to discuss a matter, they are not on campus when you need them. They are not trying to avoid you but are probably in schools visiting students, lecturing elsewhere or engaged in a research activity. It is therefore better to make an appointment which is mutually convenient. Most tutors will do their best to see you straight away, especially if the matter is urgent and, if the tutor you need is off campus, then another will probably be able to help you. Students often want to catch a tutor at the end of a teaching session to raise queries about the session, a forthcoming assignment or a school practice matter. Most tutors are willing to deal with student concerns as they arise, but their time may be limited because they have another teaching session to get to or a meeting to attend. In such circumstances, you can ask a tutor to leave you a note, telephone you or arrange to see you at a time when they can give your query the time it deserves.

You will find that, in the main, education tutors are friendly, approachable and keen to do what they can to help you. However, even in the best of all possible worlds, some tutors are more approachable and accessible than others. Students are usually very quick to sort out who is and who isn't accessible which means that the more available tutors sometimes get overburdened, so be aware of this when you join the queue to see the tutor that everyone else wants to see.

Good relationships with significant tutors can make the difference between giving up, mere survival or sustained enjoyment on the course. The following advice should help to tip the balance in favour of coping and enjoyment.

- Avoid letting a problem fester and develop into a debilitating anxiety. Go and talk about it with the relevant tutor as soon as possible. There are often more solutions or ways round problems than you think.

- It may help *you* to get a problem off your chest by offloading it as you pass your tutor in the corridor, but a rushed and hasty encounter may not give you or the tutor the best chance to give your problem the time and attention it requires. Make an appointment which will give you and your tutor a chance to think about possible resolutions beforehand. The result may be much more satisfactory.

- Because tutors have many competing claims on their time and energy, they are more likely to invest time on *your* problem if you demonstrate that you have done some constructive thinking yourself and have one or two suggestions or proposals for resolving it.

- Essay or assignment tutorials are most productive when the student has done some reading and thinking beforehand. The more you bring with you to the tutorial, including specific questions which you want answers to, the more the tutor will be able to contribute and help you. The least satisfactory tutorial for both student and tutor are those where the student arrives intellectually empty-handed with an expectation that the tutor will do their thinking for them.

- If you cannot find the tutor you need and your problem is urgent, try and find another tutor who can help. There is usually someone on campus who will be able to come to your assistance. Failing this, many tutors these days have a telephone answering service or voice-mail facility. This will enable you to leave a message.

Making sense of it all

Because everything you meet in these first few weeks is new information, it is hard to retain it all. It is in the nature of new jobs, new responsibilities and new courses in higher education that you are introduced to unfamiliar, complex learning and information systems in a very short space of time. The library and computer facilities are two sites where, however skilled and carefully paced the induction sessions are, there is simply too much information to absorb in one session. Unless you already have working experience of an academic library or a computer of your own, you have little previous, practical understanding on which to graft the new knowledge. So the incoming data will remain at a distance from your grasp until you make regular use of the facilities and learn by trial and error. In so doing, you need to set yourself realistic targets and tackle new learning in small, manageable steps. This was certainly how many of the mature students in my research survived the first week. Ann Major, for example, had early discovered that she coped best by breaking the day down into discrete units and coping with each bit as it came along:

AM It's trying not to do everything at once. It's taking little bits at a time and each day – taking each part of the day, as a unit in itself.

The Library

If, like most first year students, your previous experience of libraries has been limited to your local library or the school library, the many-storeyed library of a large university or college with its multi-media technology will be baffling at first. To begin with you will be shown where the education section is and how the shelf and book numbering system works. Much of the information about where to find books, videos and journals is now stored in on-line computers which you can use by following a fairly simple search procedure. Other, more encyclopaedic information is stored on multi-media computers which you can access via CD ROMS.[3] These disks store comprehensive listings of new book publications and all the books and journal articles on a particular topic, like behaviour management or the teaching of spelling, for example. The procedure for using CD ROMs is more complex and is probably best done with a librarian's or technician's assistance at a point when you need to use it. There are also the Internet facilities with vast networks of web-sites which include a rapidly expanding growth of educational data like Ofsted School Reports.

The information technology now available in most campus libraries is fast becoming more sophisticated and most students (and tutors for that matter), have difficulty in keeping abreast of it. The key to making sense of what should be a vital source of learning support for you, is to get into the library for short periods of time at least two or three times a week. Avoid the unhappy experience of a male student I once taught who, somewhat late in the day, took himself off to the library in a state of panic about an overdue essay, had no clear plan of what to look for or how to search for it, became totally dejected because he could not find anything he needed, was too afraid to ask a librarian for assistance in case he would be considered stupid, left empty-handed and never went back there again. Unfortunately, I did not discover this until late on in his final year when he was already seriously behind in his studies. Needless to say, he failed his course. There is no need for any student to have this kind of experience because Help Desks and other kinds of librarian assistance are always available during library opening times. However, for the purposes of the first few weeks, the following advice should get you off the starting blocks:

- Set some time aside each week to go into the library for a specific goal, like searching for one of the books on your course reading list. On the first occasion you might simply walk to the education shelves, browse around to see what's there and look for the book you want by using the alphabetical order of authors' surnames. Take the book to the issue desk and leave the library having successfully accomplished your first academic mission.

- On the second occasion, enter the library with the intention of using the on-line computer search facilities to find one of the books on your reading list. Simply follow the procedures on the screen and you will soon see how straightforward it is. This activity is best undertaken with a friend. This way you can support each other and laugh at the mistakes you make. If you get really stuck, seek help from a librarian. This is part of their job and they will be pleased to help you. Make a note of the shelf reference and book number and go and find the book. If it's out on loan request a recall. If unseccessful, go back to the search facilities and try again with another book.

- Whilst it's fresh in your mind, begin to make more frequent use of the on-line search facilities, extending it to include periodical and journal articles. Find an article you are interested in and sit down at one of the tables and read it. Get into the habit from the start of making a note of the title of the book or article, journal source, author, date and page numbers before you begin making notes. Find a system of storing this information so that you can retrieve it quickly. This way you won't have to waste precious time looking for the details of something you read weeks ago when you want to use it in an essay.

• Don't wait until your first essay is due before you make your first foray into the library. You will find to your frustration, that most of the books you want are already out on loan. Your way out of trouble is to join the queue for the short loan collection[4] but bear in mind that this is generally in heavy demand in the days running up to an essay submission date.

• Get to know who the education librarians are and introduce yourself. These people have a specialist knowledge of a whole range of educational resources, including children's literature and they can be an invaluable source of help when it comes to finding material for an essay, a research project or teaching experience.

• Make two or three trips to the section of the library which houses school books and classroom materials. Browse through the shelves and get acquainted with the way in which they are classified. This will give you a rough idea of what resources are available for loan when it comes to your first teaching practice.

Computers don't bite

We have not yet reached a point in our education system where every student arrives on the course with basic IT (Information Technology) competence. As mature students, you may have had experience of using computers at work, at school or at home. If you have, you will have some familiarity with creating and saving files, a keyboard facility and a knowledge of at least one word-processing package. This will give you a useful baseline from which to develop even though you may have to get accustomed to different machines and software. On the other hand, you may never have used a computer in your life. This is not uncommon and I know at least two widely published professors in premier league universities, who continue to shun the computer in favour of fountain-pen and notepad. However, you will not have this option in teacher education because IT or ICT (Information Communication Technology) as it is now called, is playing an increasingly important part in the National Curriculum and may well become a core subject. Many children now have access to home computers, are keyboard competent and have a basic knowledge of file-handling. They are quick to master new technological skills and teachers therefore have to be ahead of the game and sufficiently knowledgeable in ICT to enable children to learn the necessary skills to become active partici- pants in an increasingly ICT dependent world. Part of the Labour Government's pledge is to make every classroom a 'connected' class- room with access to electronic mail and the Internet. If you consider yourself to be a computer illiterate you need to accept the fact that you will have some ICT 'upskilling' to do. There is no mystique about computers. You simply have to need to use the facilities they offer and practise a little and often until you build up your technical confidence. ICT will be an important part of your training course and you will receive experienced help and guidance both from education tutors and teachers in school. However, there is insufficient time to teach all you need to know to reach the required level of ICT competence and ex- perience of software packages, so a significant amount of practice and specific tasks will need to be carried out on your own, outside taught sessions. The following, basic advice is intended for those of you who consider yourselves to be techno-phobics:

- See ICT as a new skill to be learned and approach it in the same way as you did when you first learned to drive a car. Anyone with basic intelligence can learn to use a computer. Take one small step at a time, in short bursts of activity and you will be surprised at how quickly you begin to build up a repertoire of skills and techniques.

- If you can, invest in your own computer at home. There are some good deals in the highstreet shops, if you are prepared to shop around. Nothing is so valuable as being able to practise and make mistakes in the privacy of your own home. Once you have one of your own, you will quickly wonder how you managed without it!

- Find a friend who is a bit more competent than you and agree times when you will both carry out assigned ICT tasks on campus together. In exchange, offer a quid pro quo form of help in an area in which you feel more confident than your partner. Mutual support in acknowledged areas of weakness can be an extremely valuable way of overcoming fear and inadequacy.

- Set up a small number of clear targets to achieve each week. Better to undertake a small number of new skills and procedures on a regular basis than to do nothing for several weeks and then try to cover too much ground in one session.

- There are often two or three different ways of carrying out the same procedure. Take risks and experiment with these and other facilities on the screen. Unless you throw it on the floor, the computer is very hard to 'break'.

- There are now available some very accessible guides and specific, procedural instructions which accompany software packages. Ask your tutor about the ones s/he would recommend and follow one through as part of one of your weekly targets.

Good habits in note-taking

There are plenty of books which can give you advice on how to study on prominent display in the university or college bookshop at the beginning of a new academic year. These study manuals will also include a comprehensive section on the taking and making of notes so I do not propose to repeat in this book what is probably better done elsewhere. The purpose of this section is to offer you some basic pointers on note-taking, an activity which will dominate the first term of your course. If I can help you to get into the habit of making succinct, readable notes which still make sense several months later, you will have learned an invaluable skill which will serve you well not only in your course of training but throughout your teaching career. You may be surprised to learn that, until recently, pupils frequently left school without having been taught how to make notes. It was a skill which pupils learned 'on the hoof' if at all and the question of whether they were effective or ineffective note-takers was usually the consequence of chance or natural aptitude. Many of the students I have taught have lamented their poor note-taking skills especially when it comes to examination revision or preparation for an essay. Notes they thought would be a lifeline often turned out to be virtually useless since they couldn't decipher them or couldn't make sense of them when they did! Since the introduction of the National Curriculum in 1988, teachers have been required to teach Key Stage Two pupils how to take and make notes as part of the English curriculum. Hopefully, this will mean that students will, in the future, enter courses of higher education as competent note-takers.

Listening, while simultaneously taking notes usually means that one suffers at the expense of the other or indeed, that they *both* suffer. The skill lies in the ability to take notes which are brief enough to allow you to listen carefully without losing the thread of the argument but not so brief and elliptical that you cannot make head or tail of them later. An awareness of and attention to the following should help you to develop some good note-taking habits.

- Practise listening to and taking notes of a news bulletin on the radio or television at home for a ten minute period, preferably before your course begins. Listen to a subsequent news bulletin on the same day and check how much *key* information you were able to record accurately. You should not bother to record descriptions, embellishments or details which add colour to the information you have noted. Three important questions which you should ask about your notes are: Can I read them ? Do they make sense? Do they accurately record what was reported? If the answer to any of these is negative, you need to keep practising until you get three affirmative responses.

- Aim to take notes which are clear and legible and which do not need writing up afterwards. As the pace of the course quickens, you will not have time to re-work lecture notes.

- Develop your own shorthand for high frequency words like, children, school, education, learning, teaching, behaviour etc., by drawing up a key of abbreviations. For example: Education – ed; behaviour – bhvr; children – ch. Carry the key with you for quick reference and add to it as the need arises.

- If you are given lecture summaries or outlines use them to add notes of your own. However, avoid becoming too reliant on them because not all tutors provide them.

- Do *not* try to everything down. You will lose the gist of the lecture and end up with half-finished sentences which will be no help to you when you re-visit your notes in the future. Listen instead for the key points, new concepts and main research findings and make a *brief* note of these.

- Get into the habit of writing questions in the margin as they occur to you because the most effective learning often occurs when probing questions are asked. You can follow these up later with your own further reading or raise them with your tutor.

- Underline or highlight anything which does not make sense or is not clear to you. Raise any ambiguities you have noted as soon as possible with fellow students or with the tutor in the follow-up seminar.

Feeling like a student teacher and feeling good

Halfway through the first term the mature women in my research were beginning to feel that they were acquiring a student identity. Attendance at lectures, seminars, using the library, talking about their first essays and anticipating their first school experience all helped to contribute to a sense that they had arrived as students and had begun to think of themselves as such. However, the mood swings from euphoria to anxiety which characterised their first few days continued to erupt from time to time as the reality of new routines and demands began to affect their lives at home and at college. Some women felt this emotional see-saw more keenly than others and this appeared to depend, to some extent, on their domestic circumstances. Some idea of the different ways in which individuals reacted to the initial reality of becoming a student can be seen in the following interview extracts with Beth Wells and Carole Payne:

Beth Wells
DD And how has the course so far, met your expectations?

BW Probably more exciting than I thought it would be. I don't know if I expected it to be as enthusiastic and thought provoking and um ... revolutionary almost, in some of the ideas and approaches. I didn't realise that education could be so exciting really. And I feel that all of the tutors are so enthusiastic about their subjects and I do feel filled with enthusiasm by them.

Carole Payne
DD How are things going so far?

CP Up and down I would say. I'm really enjoying it but perhaps becoming a bit overwhelmed. Just the sheer volume of having to cope with the family and really fitting everything in, so I think that's it.

Beth's two children were both settled at junior school and she received positive emotional and practical support from her husband. You will recall from the previous chapter that she had also thought very carefully about the timing of her decision to train for teaching and was very secure in her belief that the time was 'right' both for herself and her family. Carole also had firm support from her husband and children but, in addition to two boys who were both at school, she had a two year old baby daughter who was left with a child minder during the day. The demands of a young infant on top of other family responsibilities, meant that her daily routine was more complex than Beth's and this, coupled with some anxiety and conflict about being separated from her daughter, resulted in a greater preoccupation with having to 'fit everything in' than was the case for Beth. Carole's enjoyment of the early part of the course did not, therefore, have the same energetic enthusiasm.

The key to understanding how the women strove to redefine themselves as student teachers alongside their realities as mothers and wives, could only be reached by an analysis of the interrelationship between their domestic and student lives. This became a central theme in my research and some of its findings will be the focus for attention in the next chapter where I recount some of the successful and less successful strategies which the women used to juggle the increasing demands of academic and domestic responsibility.

For the time being, however, feeling like student teachers is not yet a stable perception. It was generally more strongly felt whilst they were at college during the day but were relegated to the 'back burner' when they returned home in the evening and reverted to their roles as mothers and wives. Despite the tenuous and mercurial nature of the women's grip on their emergent student teacher identity, many of them conveyed a sense of excitement about doing all the things they had imagined students did when came into higher education. The physical impedimenta of books, paper, pens and text highlighters helped to give the women a tangible sense that they were now student teachers rather as a student doctor might feel when she donned a white coat and stethoscope for the first time. These palpable signs, combined with a clearly defined sense that they were learning and making progress towards their goal of becoming a teacher, were frequently recounted with pleasure by the women. This was Pauline Cash when she identified the first time she felt like a B.Ed student:

PC ... it was a strange feeling but it was very exciting. It must have been the second week, when the school experience was on the horizon and the essays and things like that. And I really felt sort of part of it and that, you know, I'm here!

Notes

1   A view of individuals as active and creative participants in socialization rather than as passive receivers of change, is taken from the interactionist model of adaptation which Lacey (1977) used in his study of teacher socialization.

2   The term 'seminar' has three definitions: it can mean a small class at a university etc. for discussion and research; a short intensive course of study; a conference of specialists. In teacher training programmes, the first form of seminar is the one most commonly used.

3   The abbreviation CD ROM stands for Compact Disc Read Only Memory.

4   The 'short loan' collection includes core texts, usually on essential reading lists, which can be borrowed for a short period which is normally anything from an hour to twenty-four hours. This allows central texts to be accessed by a large number of students. However, failure to return the materials at the end of the stipulated time can result in heavy fines.

Chapter 3

Keeping all the plates in the air

We are all of us fabulous. We are heroic characters in stories of import, stories which contain warnings and wisdom, meanings and lessons.... The times are troubled. Valuable enterprises are cramped and confined or are shrivelling and crumbling away. Damaging projects are being let loose in their place. But there are teachers and headteachers everywhere who are continuing to hope and to embody their hope, relentlessly, fabulously, in hard work.[1]

This chapter leaves behind the first weeks of initial encounters as a student teacher to focus on the everyday reality of what it means to be a full-time student. Towards the end of the first term, the academic pressures begin to accelerate with demands for the first pieces of assessed work. This juncture was invested with considerable significance by the women since it was the first time they would be assessed according to degree criteria. The marks they received for this essay would confirm them as credible undergraduates. Thus a great deal hung on it, in terms of the tangible 'proof' it gave them about their capability, or lack of it, to succeed on the course. What kind of impact does this pressure have on the individual women and their families? As the date for essay submission draws nearer, how do mature women student teachers reconcile the domestic demands, which unfortunately do not lessen commensurably, as academic pressures increase? What strategies do they use to avoid the meeting of one obligation at the expense of the other? What changes have to take place in order to accommodate to the increased workload of a vocational degree course?

Using the experience of the women in my study as they struggled to cope with the many competing claims on their time throws light on these questions. Case studies of two women who had to surmount some protracted personal and domestic difficulties during the course illustrate how it is possible to survive and achieve academic success despite great problems. These stories of human endeavour show that courage, fortitude and intelligent use of human resources can be as important as academic and professional ability.

Reality: the pain and the pleasure

For the women in the research group, the first year was now well under way and they were fully immersed in student life. Attendance at lectures, school visits, workshop activities, and taking work home to complete had now become a routine part of their new life. Most of the women relished the training sessions at college during the day and greatly enjoyed observing children and teachers at work in schools from their new perspective as student teachers. However, part of the experience of being a student also involved the more difficult challenge of finding ways of coping with the increasing pressure of course work while holding onto periods of quality time with their husbands, partners and children. The basic chores of cooking meals, doing the washing, ironing and shopping still had to be done, but in ever decreasing amounts of time as academic work encroached further into their private lives. At the start, when the workload was lighter, most of the women tried to fit their study around the housework. Once the demand for assessed work became imminent, this was no longer possible and domestic chores had to be pared to the minimum to make way for the writing and completion of essays. One of the consequences of an increased pace of life at home was a loss of time for personal recreation and an ever present feeling of fatigue. The following extract shows how Carole Payne defined her 'new' reality:

CP ... I think I underestimated how demanding compared to the Access course, it actually is. Whilst I was prepared for the hard work here and the essays and things, it's all-consuming. It fills our whole lives really. There doesn't seem to be a moment, particularly this term when we can think about doing something else.

The perception on the part of the women that being a student was 'all consuming' was repeated graphically in the diaries which I asked them to keep for a ten-day period early in the Spring term, and record every domestic, family and college-related activity from when they woke up until they went to bed. The diaries provided another source of evidence about the impact of academic demands upon their family lives which might not otherwise have surfaced in the interviews. The following section from Carole Payne's diary demonstrates the crowded schedule of activity which had become her reality now that course had picked up speed. Carole is married with three children: Peter, Mark and Tracey aged eleven, nine and two, respectively:

Thursday 6th February, 1992

6.30	Awoke to 'Today'. Best part of the day.
6.45	Had shower while Tom (husband) made tea. Unloaded dishwasher and washing machine.
7.00	Peter and Mark up and dressed. Tracey stirring. Hung washing out. Boys set table for breakfast. Tom dresses Tracey while I make beds and clean bathrooms.
7.30	Breakfast together.
7.45	Tom leaves for work. Children clean teeth and get their bags ready. Tracey potters about helping them. I dust and hoover downstairs. Scrub potatoes and put casserole in slow cooker.
8.10	Get everyone sorted out to leave home.
8.15	Leave house. Wait for school bus to arrive. See children off.
8.25	Take Tracey to childminder and then on to college.
9.00	Maths. Great session making games.
11.00	Coffee and lunch with friends. Had good chat mostly about maths games.
12.00	Group of us met to write script for our language tape. Karen went with me to take car to garage in between work on language project. It went well.
3.00	Schools and Society lecture. Felt tired once I sat down to listen. Kept thinking about Peter and Mark. I always worry in case they forget to go to friend's house. They haven't forgotten yet!
9.00	Got science project out to decide upon tomorrow's assignment. Tom arrived home. Ate supper while I chatted about science and Tom filled me in on work.
10.30	Tom cleaned shoes while I made coffee.
10.45	Read chapter for Key Concepts.
11.15	Lay down to sleep.

The structure of Carole's day was fairly typical of the women's diary recordings. The day began early with an onslaught of domestic activity, the aim of which was to get as much housework and advanced meal preparation done as possible in order to create space at the end of the day to spend time with their children before they began to work on college assignments. Women with young children seldom made a start on their academic work before eight-thirty or nine o' clock, after the children had been settled into bed for the night. By this time their energy levels were low and, after an hour or so, they generally lost concentration, returned to more domestic chores in preparation for the next day and retired to bed. Academic work appeared to fit in around the demands of family life into whatever slots and spaces occur amidst the family routine. What is apparent from Carole's diary as well as those of several other women, is the high value they place upon spending time with their children. Being a mother and enjoying the company of their children is a pleasure which is cherished and closely guarded form competing intrusions. Also noteworthy is the part Carole's husband played in the care of the children, domestic chores and his interest in her course. Whilst it was undoubtedly the case that Carole took the major responsibility for the care of the children, it was evident from the interviews that Tom enjoyed being with the children and willingly shared many of the routine chores which underpinned their daily well-being. He had also encouraged Carole to take up teaching and his involvement and support in her academic progress was a key factor in her enjoyment of the course. This was not true for all the women; indeed, about half the husbands were conspicuous by their absence in the diary recordings. However, the emotional, practical and academic help which certain husbands gave to their student teacher wives was a particularly interesting finding and I return to it later.

The common factor in all the diaries was of overwhelming commitment to their course of teacher training and an ability to endure an extensive range of daily demands on their time and energy. The price the women pay is the virtual lack of any kind of social life and the loss of freedom to use their private time for personal leisure. Pamela Jones makes this point abundantly clear:

PJ... I mean this diary reads ... all it ever says is fill the washing machine, empty the tumble dryer and iron the clothes. There isn't actually any time in the whole ... I think it was twelve days I managed to complete it ... there isn't any time in the whole twelve days when I've done anything for me. I mean I might have sat down for about five minutes and collapsed in a chair with a cup of coffee but I've got no social life according to this diary, whatsoever.

By the middle of the second term of the first year, the reality of being a student had made a significant impact upon the women's lives. It had penetrated most aspects of their private lives, accelerating the tempo of their daily routines into a treadmill of constant activity.

If you are beginning to think that this reality is one you can do without, remember that these are individual snapshots of the women's subjective feelings as they encountered the first wave of academic pressure. Pamela Jones, for example, was one of the course's most enthusiastic advocates and is currently a very successful teacher who loves every minute of her work. Despite the mounting pressure of essay deadlines and forthcoming examinations, most of the women spoke animatedly about the enjoyment, challenge and stimulation they were getting from the course. Moreover, they spoke of the positive changes which had taken place in their self-esteem and in their identities as individuals, as the following comments exemplify:

> ... I just love it. I just love the whole atmosphere, everything. (Carole Payne)

> ... I'm much more confident now and cope with things better now. No, I enjoy the fact that this is doing something for my benefit. Not purely on a selfish level but just because I'm actually living life again. I'm not living life through other people which is what as a mother with little children, you're very much doing. People here know me as 'me', not with my children or with my husband – here it's me! (Christine Kift)

The experience of being a student from the mature women's perspective is rather like the curate's egg, partly good and partly bad. The curriculum in the second term is challenging but difficult. They enjoy the demands made upon them to think about abstract ideas but dread the examinations. They acknowledge the gains made in their self-confidence and welcome the stirrings of a new identity which education is opening up for them. But this is won at the expense of a loss of time for their own personal leisure. They want to complete assignments on time and do well in them but they do not wish to relinquish time spent with their children.

You can cope: strategies for survival

The word 'coping' is sometimes erroneously associated with just get-ting by, a kind of make-do-and-mend approach to situations of chal-lenge and difficulty. In fact, it means the effective and successful management of people, problems or tasks.[2] What the women in my research did was to find specific ways of coping which were not only successful in terms of their particular needs but which were also *creative* responses to the problems that faced them at the time. When coping actions become repeated responses to conflicting tensions or moments of crisis which resolved problems as well as reduced conflict, I call them 'coping strategies'. The concept of coping strategies became a key mechanism for understanding and explaining how the women changed and adapted to the student teacher role. Before I dis-cuss some of the coping strategies which the women used to manage the escalating demands on their time, I need to explain the source of this concept.

In 1982, Andrew Pollard, a sociologist working in the field of educa-tion, conducted some research on classroom coping strategies which shed light on how teachers and pupils negotiated relationships which acted to maintain a degree of harmony in what he termed, a 'working consensus' in the classroom.[3] His main argument was that teachers and pupils have specific sets of interests which need to be satisfied if both parties are to survive in what can be a stressful environment in terms of noise, personal threat, high numbers of pupils and the need for successful learning to take place. For teachers, a crucial element in their coping strategies springs from a desire to defend themselves from personal threat and in classrooms the aspects of self-interest most likely to be threatened are defined by Pollard as self-image, work-load, health and stress, enjoyment, autonomy, order and instruction (1982, p.32). Depending on the individual biography of the teacher, some aspects of these self-interests will have greater prominence than others and teachers will respond by using what Pollard calls 'strategic defen-sive adaptations' to protect themselves (p.32). This leads Pollard (1985) to define coping strategies as 'a creative but semi-routinised and situational means of protecting the individual's self' (p.155).

Because the women in the study frequently referred to their own subjective definitions of coping, this concept applied particularly well to the changes they were making in their own lives as student teachers. Their self-interests included the need to protect the time they wished to spend with their families, their need to preserve the basic essentials of an ordered, domestic routine and their wish to achieve success as student teachers. Prominence in one or other of these self-interests came to the fore according to what was considered most important at the time. Successful coping strategies were those which served their combined interests as mothers and students whilst at the same time reducing the ever present conflict between the two. However, coping strategies cannot be used like cook-book recipes which work for all users provided the instructions are followed. They differ according to biography and family circumstances and the choice of strategy is dependent on the available personal and financial resources of the individual. A case study of one of the women in the research group will serve to illustrate what coping strategies 'look' like as well as putting them into a human context.

Pat Grade

At the time of the study Pat was thirty-one and married with three children. Before enrolling on the B.Ed course she had been a 'dinner lady' and parent-helper at her children's primary school. She was warm and ebullient with a ready wit and sense of humour which quickly ensured her popularity with tutors and student peers. The point at which we pick up Pat's story is a few weeks into the Spring term. The first essays were in the process of being returned and the end of year examinations in April/May, were on the horizon.[4] These were the cause of considerable anxiety because without a satisfactory pass in all subjects, no student could proceed to the second year and they were especially worrying for the mature students who had not sat a formal examination for many years.

Pat's husband, Alan, who had agreed to take on a larger share of domestic responsibility and child care once Pat became a full-time student, had suffered a back injury as a result of a sporting accident and was in hospital when she got the marks for her first three essays. She had done well with two essays, having gained marks of 65% and 63%, both of which fall within the 2.1 degree classification band.[5] But she was devastated by the relatively low mark which she achieved for her third essay and, despite her customary, upbeat attitude to life, she was on the point of considering giving up the course:

> Then we had the Primary Curriculum one (essay) and I only had 48% for that and that really knocked the feet from under me and I had that week before Alan went into hospital – and when he went in, I said, I don't know if I really want to carry on. Is there any point? And I had a long talk to my Primary Curriculum tutor[6] who said, don't worry about this. But to me it was a sort of warning, if you like. The tutor kept saying 48% was a pass mark and I shouldn't worry about it, but to me, it was a low mark and it wasn't good enough.

Pat may not originally have set herself the goal of maintaining a 2.1 mark profile, but, like many of the women, once they had glimpsed its possibility by the early achievement of good marks, they were very keen to sustain them (see Appendix pp.133). Subsequent reductions in their marks came as a considerable disappointment and her tutor may not have given sufficient credence to Pat's high expectations of herself. Pat's distress was not, however, solely attributable to one low essay mark. She had a heavy family burden, with three young children and had entered the course with the expectation that her husband would take on a greater share of domestic responsibilities. His back injury at an early point in her first year meant that she lost the help she had depended upon. Sadly, as the year progressed, her family difficulties worsened. Alan's back condition deteriorated and initial hopes for his recovery faded. After months of absence from work, Alan eventually lost his job[7] and, as his illness intensified, his mobility became increasingly restricted. The 'warning' which Pat spoke of signalled her fear that she would have to cope with academic and family demands on her own. Indeed, her husband's virtual immobility meant that he now needed care and help, so her responsibilities at home became greater. If she achieved what she considered an unsatisfactory mark before any of these straitened circumstances had really begun to bite, how would this bode for future marks, now that she was so much more burdened at home? In order for Pat to meet these increased demands as well as keep abreast of academic work, any coping strategies she devised would have to be supremely efficient of her truncated time and energy. In addition, they would be heavily constrained by financial restrictions now that Alan was unemployed, on top of which was the mounting pressure to do well and succeed on the course since she was likely to become the sole earner in the family.

The plight in which Pat found herself aptly illustrates the point I made earlier about the necessity for successful coping strategies to align closely with the particular circumstances of the individual. In this case, economic, family, academic and biographical factors combined to influence the strategies which she came to use. The way in which she managed to juggle the many claims upon her time would become crucial to her survival on the course and the following extracts indicate clearly the coping strategies which she had begun to operate. I asked her firstly how she managed to keep on top of essay deadlines:

> Well, everyone asks me this. The thing I've always done as soon as I get an assignment, I check through what's the assignment and I begin to build ideas straight away. I go straight away to the library because everyone usually leaves it to the end and that's when all the books have gone.

DD So you do the spade work straight away?

> Oh yes. I have to because if I left it all to the end it would be too much at once so I just take great big quotes out the book and write them down. So, I've been using essay tutorials as opportunities to say, 'Well, I've included this, this and this. Is that relevant? And they say, 'Fine.'

Pat had quickly learned that early visits to the library, preferably on the first or second day of receiving the essay titles, paid off. At this point in her husband's illness, Alan was on half-pay and book purchase was a luxury she could no longer afford. She therefore had to depend upon the college library for her supply of books. Her days were now so tightly packed with activity that no more could be squeezed into them; she dare not risk leaving the writing of an essay too close to the deadline because there would be insufficient time to do justice to it. So her strategy was to make a start on it as soon as possible so that she could work on it in manageable chunks of time whilst at the same time, keeping on top of her family commitments. One of the benefits of this advanced organisation was that she was able to use the essay tutorials to check and confirm that she was on the right lines as far as content and essay structure was concerned.[8] Pat's family circumstances limited the strategies available to her and sharpened her need to make maximum use of college facilities and uncommitted periods of time between lectures and workshops when other students might have taken time out to socialise with their friends. The pressures which now bore down upon Pat meant that she had to maximise whatever 'bits' of time came her way. She spoke a great deal about 'snatching', 'catching', and 'grabbing' time. There were simply never enough stretches of time in any one day for her to schedule time to give her the uninterrupted periods of quiet concentration which are often needed for productive, intellectual work. The ability to make the best use of whatever odd moments of time came her way became a key survival strategy. This was clear from her explanation to me about how she found the time to prepare and revise for the forthcoming, end of year, examinations:

> It was snatched, a lot if it. If I was lucky I would get a whole hour, if not it'd be half an hour or even quarter of an hour. If I only learned one trigger word in a quarter of an hour, I'd think, at least it's something, I'm on my way. It was snatched when I could do it.

Pat's preparedness to make effective use of fifteen minutes in order to achieve the smallest of goals, gives another insight into why the strategy worked for her when it might not have done so for others. She had a positive and resilient personality which enabled her to feel that she was making progress even if it meant that she only learned one key word. A student without Pat's buoyant disposition might have considered the achievement too minimal to comment upon, let alone feel that s/he was making sound progress towards exam preparation. Pat's strategies showed a solid, pragmatic approach to problems and creative capacity to make the best use of what resources she had at her disposal. In the next extract Pat is describing the method she used for exam revision:

> My method is – I suppose it's the wrong way to revise. I just take chunks of things and really condense them down to the smallest amount of words that I can, that will still retain the meaning. And then I just learn them 'parrot-fashion' and when I feel I've learned them, I write down what I know. My eldest daughter helps me. I put them on postcards and I just read out to her what's on the postcard. So at the beginning of the exam I wrote down all that I knew in pencil at the front of the exam paper, and then I just rearranged it. And I felt that really helped.

Pat went on to explain that she had learned 'trigger' words or headings which she claimed, 'sparked off the bumph which went with them.'

Much of the examination revision had to be carried out during the Easter vacation which immediately preceded the beginning of the Summer term when the exams took place. For mature students with families this was a most unsuitable study period because the children were at home at the same time. Use of time therefore had to be carefully planned in ways which did not conflict too strongly with competing interests. Pat's response to this difficulty was to reduce potential conflict by involving her eldest daughter. This creative use of family resources would also have had the effect of making her daughter feel that she was making an important contribution to her mother's academic progress to say nothing of the positive role model it was giving her about the importance of commitment and tenacity in the achievement of an academic and vocational aspiration.

Pat was equally creative in the way she resolved the substantial domestic burden she had to carry on her own by involving her children in a share of the routine household chores:

> ...I'm a great one for rotas. I give the children rotas, They have to have certain responsibilities. I've told them if you want to help me to stay at college you've got to do some of this. So they do their own lunch boxes. They keep their bedrooms tidy and I do a routine check. I'll take up the hoover for them and they'll take it in turns to hoover their bedrooms and one of them will hoover my bedroom.

According to Pat, her children fully understood how important it was for their mother to be able to complete her B.Ed course so that she could eventually earn a much needed income, and they willingly took on a share of domestic responsibilities. Pat took out an 'insurance' against the onset of tedium on the part of her children, by organising a rotation of jobs so that they each took a turn in doing different tasks.

It would be easy to be critical of Pat's snatch-and-grab raids on time as a means of making academic progress on an intensive degree course. Her methods for essay writing and examination revision are, perhaps, crude and her claim to be able to use 'trigger' words to 'spark off the bumph that went them', verges on the comical. But Pat's refreshingly candid account of how she survived these pressures in the context of her husband's increasing disability and job loss, in fact, reveals a very efficient and creative coping strategy which worked to serve her interests. From her perspective, her priority was to pass the first year examinations so that she could continue with the course while meeting the complex and time consuming needs of her family. She could not afford to spend large amounts of time away from the family and there was no other adult or family member on whom she could shift some of the domestic load. She therefore reduced potential guilt and conflict within the family by enlisting the help of her eldest child in memorising key words and headings to help her recall some of their associated theories and concepts and this proved an effective memory retrieval system which served her well in the examination. The constraints of limited time and available energy are negotiated through her family, the needs of which strongly influenced the strategies she was able to use. She was also having to manage on a tight budget and so could not afford baby sitters, paid domestic help or any of the hardware of study, like book purchase or a personal computer which might have made her life a little easier. She therefore adapted to these constraining factors by scaling down the revision enterprise to postcard-size, which had the merit of being both physically and psychologically manageable. In this way her prominent needs as a student were met, albeit in a rough-hewn manner, without sacrificing the needs of her family.

Pat's pragmatic and realistic approach to the problems which beset her forced her to lower her academic expectations. I subsequently labelled Pat's particular coping strategy, '*strategic pragmatism*'. As the course progressed, she honed these coping strategies so that they became a highly efficient and routinised part of her student life. A clear testimony to their success was Pat's graduation with a 2.1 degree, a remarkable achievement given the severity of the problems which beset her throughout the course.

Tackling the first essay: a survivor's guide

Because this essay is not simply about marks but more about the rite of passage into legitimate studenthood, its significance can become inflated to the point where the very thought of having to do it brings dread and self doubt. In order to avoid these feelings from getting out of proportion to the task in hand, the following guidance should help you on this crossing of the Rubicon. Many of the practical approaches used by Pat to get over this academic hurdle make sound sense and are well worth heeding, some of which are incorporated below.

- Avoid the temptation to put off the moment you intend to commence work on the essay. Getting started is often the hardest part of writing an essay. Once you begin work you feel less anxious and when the ideas begin to hang together, you may even enjoy writing it! Begin by reading the essay title very carefully making sure you understand what is meant by it. Discuss your ideas with others. There are often at least two or three elements within the essay title, each of which you will need to consider.

- Gather together all the books, articles and notes that you will need for writing. Break down the reading and thinking stage into small, manageable steps. Make a timetable of what you are going to read and when and try to stick to it. Set yourself a deadline for the preparation stage so that you are not tempted to use reading as a displacement activity for writing. Remember that you are required to write an essay of some 2,000 to 3,000 words. You are not writing a book or a doctoral thesis, so you will not be expected to know all there is to know about the subject or problem in question.

- Make systematic notes along the lines I suggested in the note-making section.

- Discuss your ideas with student friends and anyone in the family who is prepared to listen. If you have to explain your ideas to them it will help to clarify your thinking.

- When you have used up the time you have allocated for the preparation stage you are ready to begin writing. Make yourself another timetable which breaks down the writing stage into small units. These might include the essay plan, introductory paragraph, development of your main argument (this might include 3 or 4 sections) and conclusion. Aim to do at least one of these units each day. This way, you will feel that you are making tangible progress.

- Before you write your essay plan, think about what it is you want to say including which conclusions you want to reach. Write down a brief statement (putting your argument in a nutshell) of what you intend to communicate, perhaps listing the main points to be made.

- From this brief statement you should be able to construct a more detailed essay plan. Because you now have some concrete ideas about the content and overall shape of your essay; this is a good moment to seek an essay tutorial.

- Work out the best order for presenting your main points. Make an outline plan of your essay indicating where you wish to insert quotations or ideas gleaned from books or lecture notes. Do not worry if you don't stick to your essay plan. Other ideas and thoughts will come into play once you start writing and these may alter your structure. If this happens, it is a sign that you are engaging with the writing process.

- Check that the ideas you want to present follow on logically from one another. If they don't, add linking ideas.

- Write the conclusion or concluding paragraphs. At this point you may wish to emphasise some points or return to the main threads in your argument but avoid repeating verbatim what you have already written elsewhere.

- If you have time at this point, lay your essay aside for two or three days. Then, when you are at some distance from it, read it through checking that you have fully addressed the main points of the essay title. Check too for accuracy in spelling, grammar and punctuation. If you know you have weaknesses in the area of written accuracy, ask someone who *is* secure in written English to read it through for you. It is also a good idea to get another person who knows very little about the subject to read your essay. If s/he understands the main argument of your essay, you have communicated well; if s/he is confused or unclear about what you are trying to say, the chances are that you have not explained your ideas sufficiently clearly and you may need to re-draft one or two paragraphs.

- Complete the final draft making any amendments. Write up the bibliography; this is an exacting task which often takes more time than you think. Careful attention to referencing and listing bibliographical details are an important part of intellectual craftsmanship so give yourself time to get it right. Finally, check that you have kept within the prescribed word limit (most institutions stipulate a marking penalty if you overshoot the limit too widely).[9]

There are other less structured approaches to essay writing where an essay plan emerges after writing freely on paper or on screen for some time. In the end it doesn't matter which approach you choose as long as it fits well with your way of thinking, working and writing. What is important is that whichever method you adopt, helps to get you started and see the writing process through to completion.

Coping with examinations

Very few people escape the nervous tension which accompanies the thought of having to sit a written examination. The dread which dogs most people is that their mind will go completely blank once they turn over the exam paper whilst the clock steadily ticks away. In fact, this rarely happens but this was small comfort to the women in my study who found the time before and during the examination period the most stressful point of the first year. Having to grapple with exam revision when you have few distractions to disturb your concentration is bad enough, but to have to revise at the same time as caring for children and running a home, is infinitely more difficult. However, a great deal of hard work and commitment had so far been invested in the course; they could not afford to lose their heads now, so it was paramount that they found ways of surmounting, what was for them, the hardest hurdle of the year.

The coping strategies they used during this arduous time were varied and depended, to some extent, on the help, support and understanding they received from the family. For example, some women made intricate, weekly revision plans with clearly specified daily goals. Others used the friendship groups they had established at college and shared out the topics for revision between them, coming together before and during the Easter vacation, to pool ideas and insights. Finding networks of support which work can be crucial during times of crisis often making the difference between swimming and sinking. One woman took her young family off to her sister's home and rented a holiday cottage nearby thus enabling her to study in peace whilst being near enough for her to reach her children quickly, should the need arise. Another took her books and notes on a family skiing holiday. She spent the day skiing with her husband and children and then, when she returned to the hotel at the end of the day, her husband took the children swimming whilst she revised for two hours before dinner in the evening. Faced with a household of family relatives to entertain throughout the Easter vacation, one woman joined her relatives for the morning's activities, began the preparation for lunch and then took herself off to her bedroom for an hour's revision each day before lunch. Her guests understood the importance of this hour to her future success on the course, took care of her two children and made sure she was not interrupted. She managed to keep to this routine of one hour's concentrated revision each day throughout the 'holiday' period and performed extremely well in the examinations.

Some of the ideas which I gleaned from the women's accounts about the methods they use to revise productively, along with some other strategies which I have shared with students over the years, may also be helpful to others.

Strategies for examination revision

*   Most institutions these days offer students revision workshops in the weeks running up to the examination period. If you know that examinations pose particular problems for you, make use of them. Students often find them very helpful.

*   A little revision done on a regular basis over a few weeks is far more effective than trying to cram in an indigestible load a few days before the exams.

*   Work with a friend by sharing out the topics to be examined, between you. This way you can pool insights, understanding and ideas.

*   Get hold of past exam papers and work through some of the questions on your own or with a friend. Most college and university libraries keep a stock of these.

*   If writing to a timed limit is one of your difficulties, set an alarm clock at home and see how much you can write about a topic or in answer to a past question, in an hour or less. Practice at timed writing will make you feel more confident when you enter the exam room.

*   Whether you are working on your own, with a friend or small group, give yourself plenty of breaks and rewards. Two of the women in my study worked for an hour together and then did a newspaper crossword over a cup of coffee as a break and diversion. An hour of actively engaged, concentrated revision is often more effective than two or three hours of fatigued effort. Try to get into the habit of working for an hour and then having a walk, cycle or swim or simply relax by listening to the radio or watching the television. Then, if you feel able to do another hour, promise yourself a different reward at the end.

*   Physical exercise is particularly important during a stressful period. Don't let it get squeezed out, however strong the temptation. If you can balance intense mental work with the exercise of your choice, you will sleep more deeply and be refreshed for another spell of work, the next day.

*   Repeated reading of the same texts and notes in the hope of imprinting them on your memory, can become tedious and stultifying with a rapidly diminishing return. Keep your interest in what you are revising alive and fresh by reading new material on the same topics. Talk about the ideas you are reading about with interested friends or relatives; this will give you some idea of how well you understand them.

*   Avoid panic revision the night before an exam. All too often it only serves to increase the panic and anxiety. Try to free the evening for a relaxing walk or the viewing of a favourite video. Go to bed early and, if you need something to get you to sleep, read something light and totally unrelated to the exams.

Networks of support

'Support' is an overused word these days, often amounting to little more than well-intentioned gestures and words which look and sound good but which are seldom followed up with actions which might have some meaning for the recipient. What I mean by support in the context of mature women trying to balance pressing domestic and academic responsibilities, is emotional, practical and academic help which is underpinned by *deeds*. Those women who were fortunate enough to receive such support were singularly advantaged over others. Gail Prince, for example, was particularly privileged insofar as she possessed a high level of both material and family resources. She had a well-equipped study, personal computer and was able to purchase all the books she needed. She could keep her domestic chores to the minimum by paying for help with the cleaning and the ironing. Her husband, who was a successful solicitor, encouraged her, read, discussed, photocopied and bound her essays. He also did all her photocopying of essential articles and teaching practice materials and took the main responsibility for cooking the family meals. He enjoyed spending time with their two children and, while she took the main responsibility for taking them to and from school, he took over at weekends leaving her free to study without interruption. This is not to suggest that Gail's adjustment to the student role was without its problems or tensions. However, compared with the women who had a range of taxing family difficulties, financial problems and husbands who could not or would not offer any form of support, her student adaptation was likely to have been a smoother and far less fraught experience than those with significantly less material and family resources. With few worries about financial restrictions, Gail had a far greater range of coping strategies at her disposal. She also had the practical and emotional support of her husband, who understood what the pressures of academic study were like from his own experience as a law student. Not only did he free her from domestic responsibilities at weekends but he also proof-read and commented upon the academic content of her essays. Those women whose husbands had experienced higher education themselves were a particularly advantaged and privileged group. Husband graduates understood the stresses involved in essay writing and revising for examinations so that the emotional support they were able to give was informed by their knowledge and 'in house' academic experience.

Christine Kift, for example, warmly acknowledged the help and academic interest which her husband took in her essays:

CK ... He's a very good sounding board as well. If I write an essay I always give it to him to read because if he can understand it, then I've said what I need to say. He may not understand some of the terms completely, but at least it makes sense and it's relevant ... It's quite good to have an objective view. It's very helpful that his standard of education or whatever, is high, because I can trust his judgement. If he says, 'That's not good enough,' then I know he's right. He's very picky on grammar and things like that.

The picture which emerged from the women who experienced this form of support was of an enriched and enhanced family life due to the sharing and involvement of husbands in their wives' experience of higher education. Christine makes the point well:

CK ... and I think also involving him makes it easier because it's not as if we're going off in two different directions which was one of the concerns we had. We keep together this way, we keep going.

But what about those women who haven't got husbands who provide solid and consistent help like these two? What of the women whose husbands resent their wives' absorption and diversion of energy into a degree course? How do women who are lone parents and have no help with childcare or household chores manage? Their need for support is even greater, given the domestic burden and financial difficulties they have to face. Do such women do less well? Whilst it is difficult to make causal connections about the relationship between academic success and resource provision in a small sample of women in one institution of higher education, if the degree results alone were taken as an indicator, the answer appears to be no, since women from both advantaged and comparatively disadvantaged groups, achieved 2.1 degree classifications (see Appendix, pp.133).

There was, however, considerable evidence in the interview data to suggest that women who had family difficulties combined with financial problems, had to pay a higher price for their success in terms of the toll it took on their own emotional and physical resources. This was true for a number of women, particularly those whose resource provision worsened during the course of the first year as their lives changed in significant respects. For example, one women's husband became bankrupt, which led to a chain of escalating financial difficulties, eventually resulting in the repossession of their home. Two women separated from their husbands and became dependent on Income Support as their main financial resource. In both cases, the women had to supplement their income by working part-time during evenings and weekends. Several others experienced the effects of a deepening economic recession in which their husbands had their working week and salaries reduced. Whilst many of the financial crises which some of the women found themselves facing were attributable to the national economic decline of the early 1990s, several were in debt by the end of the year as a result of giving up paid employment to become full-time students.[10]

Although their coping strategies were circumscribed by their limited material resources, these women, like Pat Grade, found ingenious ways of managing to keep buoyant and on top of their course work. Ultimately, they could only do what was possible in the time that was left after other commitments had been met. This meant scaling down both academic and domestic work to the bare essentials in order to survive.

Take the case of Diane Young, whose marriage broke down in her first term leaving her to cope with not only the trauma of marital separation but with learning how to become a lone parent with its attendant financial difficulties. I labelled her two main coping strategies: *strategic task reduction* and *strategic pragmatism*.

> DY ... I find it very difficult to keep up with the reading, both as far as time and fatigue are concerned. By the end of the day it's ... whether it's because I'm trying to fill two roles at home as well as this, I don't know but I tend to do just the essential reading and none of the extended reading. So really, I'm cutting myself down to two books. Well, I just can't fit it in any other way.

For students like Diane, the support of friends and family became a crucial resource. The two single parents and the women who had little help and support at home from their husbands acknowledged the importance of friendship groups at college, with whom they could share hopes, disappointments, worries and laughter. But of greatest value was the practical help they gave one another. For example, some of these friendship groups organised a book sharing facility whereby they would take it in turns to go into the library, find the key texts for an essay or examination revision topic and circulate them round the group. This made efficient use of scarce resources in the library as well as providing a common set of texts from which they could share each other's interpretations. A further advantage of this strategy was its economic use of time. They took turns in paying for the photocopying of essential materials, which were shared with the rest of the group. A telephone network was set up which enabled them to discuss how they were tackling essays or assignment projects. If one of the group's members was ill or their child unwell enough to keep them at home, one of the group would take notes and collect handouts for them. During vacation periods they would meet up in one another's homes bringing their children to play together while they pooled ideas for a teaching practice placement, exam revision or responses to essays. When one of the women felt low the group would listen and sympathise, offering comfort and any practical help they could. Most importantly, they kept each other going. During times of crisis, the group became an important sanctuary to which they knew they could turn when they needed to. The knowledge that the rest of the group was holding on and coping with the course inspired then to more determined efforts when they were jaded and downcast. Indeed, the close network of friendship and succour became such a stable and important reference point that one woman, who was having a particularly distressing time at home, told me that she would see the course through, no matter what, because her loyalty to the group made her feel that she couldn't let them down.

Another source of highly valued support was provided by relatives outside the immediate family, especially parents and parents-in-law. Several women relied heavily on their mothers, in particular, to look after their children at times when they had to be away from home. This form of help was used frequently by women who had to take up part-time work in order to meet essential expenses whilst on the course. When Barbara Melling's husband became bankrupt and redundant, they were often unable to pay the mortgage and, for a time, Barbara's mother not only paid the mortgage, but regularly sent her sums of money to help keep the family afloat when their situation was at its worst. Despite this gruelling time, Barbara told me repeatedly how glad she was that she was on the course. She was convinced that without it she would not have coped so well. When she was at college or in schools, she was so absorbed that she temporarily forgot about her troubles. The course helped her to keep a sense of perspective and gave her a much needed goal to work for, which she believed would one day help to lift the family out of financial crisis and restore their lives to normality. Barbara eventually moved to a smaller rented house which, with the help of income support, they were better able to afford. Her husband and son aged eleven involved themselves in her course and did whatever they could to help at home throughout the four years of her training. She inevitably became very tired at moments of intense pressure, but with consistent family support, her own tenacity and determination, she achieved her ambition and graduated as a qualified teacher with a 2.2 degree

There were a number of other cases where parents provided financial support during times of crisis. Despite the fact that most of the women were in their thirties and early forties, parents figured prominently in many of the women's lives and continued to be an important source of comfort and support. In addition to the practical help they received, the women spoke warmly of the interest parents took in their course and many said how much it mattered to be able to share with them the ups and downs of their progress as student teachers.

Guilt and greedy institutions

Cultural expectations of motherhood and the persistence of gender differences in our society continue to assign the main responsibility for childcare to women. As a consequence, when a conflict of interest occurs between a woman's work and the needs of her children, guilt is often the outcome. One of the difficulties in the women's attempt to keep 'all the plates in the air' was that their lives were so tightly structured that there was no slack in the system to absorb additional burdens. Any 'extra' demands on their time were likely to bring the plates crashing down. Conflict was often at its sharpest when a child was ill and there were taught sessions at college which they felt they should not miss. If they went to college, they would feel guilty for sending their children to school feeling unwell: if they stayed at home to look after them, they would feel guilty about neglecting their studies. Neither interest of self as student or self as mother could be satisfied on these occasions: it was a no-win situation and a common experience for the mature women students.

There are no easy solutions to what can be done to mitigate the effects of guilt on women but a step in the right direction is to recognise that it is not simply a personal problem but one which is widely experienced by women who combine full-time work with motherhood. Secondly, part of its pervasiveness is that it is not simply a psychological problem operating at the level of the individual; it is also mediated by the wider cultural norms of a society which continues to expect women to shoulder the main responsibility for childcare. In other words, women can be made to feel guilty through the individual psychological relationship with their child and family and through other institutions like the media, church and government who may communicate a particular moral or ethical position about where a woman's priorities should be with respect to motherhood. Consider for example, the critical reaction of a section of the American public and its associated media coverage, with respect to Matthew Eappen's mother, a medical practitioner, in the Louise Woodward case,[11] about her decision to leave her baby in the charge of an eighteen-year old paid nanny. Whilst the sharper edge of this criticism was directed at the couple's preparedness to leave their baby and hyperactive young son in the charge of an unqualified nanny to whom they paid low rates, it was nevertheless the case that two high status, professional people were subject to criticism about their childcare arrangements, even when they had lost their child.

Because opinion, in its widest sense, is still divided about the expectations of motherhood in relation to work, it is not difficult to see why guilt continues to be such a prominent part of women's experience in their attempts to juggle the competing pressures of family and work. There now exists a growing literature on the powerful way in which guilt can undermine the opportunities available to women to pursue career development and higher education. Higher education and the family can be excessively demanding on women's time and energy and the sociologist, Sandra Acker, has aptly described them both as 'greedy institutions' which claim undivided loyalty from their participants.[12] It has also been argued that families are especially greedy for women, 'requiring their constant allegiance and availability to cater to all physical and emotional needs in a way that is not required of men.'[13]

Guilt is an unpleasant sensation and women seem, for the reasons mentioned above, to be particularly prone to its influence. It is important, therefore, to remember that it is commonly experienced by women, regardless of social class background and it has its roots in cultural expectations of women's role in society as a whole. If it is inflated by other anxieties and allowed to assume a larger proportion than it merits, it can be debilitating and harmful to one's emotional health and well being. I make these points because many are likely, at some point during their teacher training, to feel its effects. All one can do in these circumstances is to act according to ones conscience and make your decision about whether childcare or academic pressures win out on the basis of what one believes to be right for that particular moment. Feelings of guilt alone should not be allowed to determine or dictate the longer term achievement of one's goal. This would only serve to perpetuate the powerful hold it has long had over the thoughts and actions of women who have wanted to better their career prospects and enhance the quality of their lives. One possible antidote to its effects would be to keep in mind the positive, longer term gains to self-esteem and the benefits to the family of a relatively secure income as a qualified teacher.

Some of the women in my study spoke enthusiastically about the way in which their course of teacher training had enhanced and enriched their family lives. Children were keen to be involved in discussions about their mother's experiences in the classroom, willingly helped to make and try out teaching materials and were proud of the fact that their mother would, one day, be a teacher. Apart from some teething problems at the beginning of the course and predictable problems about the loss of time for leisure and relaxing with the family, I heard few reports from the women that their children had suffered in any way as a result of their teacher training course. For the most part, and provided that children were kept in the picture and involved in their mother's new life as a student teacher, they quickly adjusted to the new routines and claims on their mother's time.

However, things seldom run smoothly in family life and just when you think you have established a workable system which fits with both your needs and those of your family, a crisis or clash of competing pressures will test your coping strategies to their limit. This sometimes calls for some assertive and clearly stated re-negotiation on your part.

Negotiating change

By the third term of the first year, many of the women were beginning to enjoy their new identity as student teachers and to feel that it was now a more stable and less fluctuating part of their self image. Associated with this developing student identity was greater confidence in their academic ability which was reinforced by good essay marks and positive tutor feedback about their contribution to seminar discussions. The benefits to their personal sense of worth of this developing academic confidence were highly cherished and became a closely protected part of their self-interest alongside their existing interests as mothers and wives. One of the signs that the women were making progress in their belief in themselves as student teachers was their preparedness to protect their student interests from family demands which might have threatened their academic progress. These signs, or turning points, in their student teacher socialisation appeared to be determined by the ability of the women to negotiate change both in their families and in themselves. Given their greater confidence, increased self-esteem, newly acquired skills and knowledge, confirmation in their ability to teach, and a renewed belief in themselves as individuals, this emergent student teacher identity became a prized and prominent feature of their self-interest. Its value to the women was so high that it became too precious to be relinquished. When it was threatened by family conflicts and crises, they negotiated to protect and defend their interests. In some cases the successful negotiation required a determined and unequivocal stance, especially at times when the stakes were high, as they were during the two weeks of the examination period. In the following extract Christine Kift explains the strategy she used when she felt the family's demands might interfere with her need to be in a calm frame of mind before an examination:

CK Basically I used to leave home at seven in the morning and go and have cup of coffee with one of the girls who lives in a student house and just let the family get on with it because I couldn't cope with the hassles of breakfast. So I laid it on the line to them before I started that this was how it was going to be and if they didn't like it, well that was just too bad – because this was what I'd been working for all year and if I blew this, then the whole of the rest of the year was a complete waste of time.

As Christine found, there are times when you have to be absolutely clear and single-minded about your academic commitments. Allowing the family to encroach upon the time and space she needed to prepare for the exams could have lessened her chances of doing well. She had worked hard throughout the year, had achieved a high standard of work and was not prepared to sacrifice any of the gains she had made in her successful student identity. Her husband and children recognised this, respected her wishes and made no objection to her absence at breakfast for a few days. They accepted and understood that she was now a student teacher as well as a wife and mother. Her's and the family's belief in her new identity had not been a smooth or unproblematic experience but had occurred in fits and starts throughout the year. There was the odd, minor family crisis, usually when she was under pressure with college work, domestic burdens and the need to boost the family income by part-time work as a carer in a nursing home, when she felt they weren't pulling their weight. At such times she 'laid it on the line to them' and reminded them of her need for support in the form of practical help in the home. She thus constantly negotiated and re-negotiated strategies which enabled her to balance the many demands on her time. She was an effective negotiator and so kept the family with her and managed to reduce potential conflict to a minimum. Christine was one of several mature students who, in my view, had successfully adapted to the student teacher role and there was every sign that she had constructed coping strategies which worked for herself and the family and which would see her through the rest of the course:

CK   You always start off something very tight, everything's got to be just so. But now I find that I can let things go. There are evenings when I can sit and watch the television as long as I've done an hour or two (of work). I don't spend all evening like I did to begin with ... it's probably easier than I thought ... for me to cope ... not that the course is easier, but I can cope better, I'm finding I can cope ... I do like the fact that I'm coping with it. I'm using the ability I've got rather than letting it all go. I think I'm more selfish now, but happier.

Christine was able to identify how she had changed during the year. At the end of her first year, she was more relaxed and in greater control of her life. She no longer felt the need to work long hours every evening since she had found strategies which enabled her to work more efficiently and which left her time to relax with the family in front of the television. She had 'lightened up' in every respect, to the extent that she now felt happier. She was using her undoubted academic ability, performed very well in the examinations achieving high marks and could spend more time with her family who had now adjusted to her new life as a student teacher. Her determination to do well and not allow her families' claims on her time and energy to dwarf her own needs, is however, seen critically rather than positively. Like many women she believed that it was acceptable for her to service the needs of others but 'selfish' to satisfy her own. Whether she was selfish or justifiably single-minded, the important point is that she succeeded in asserting her student needs when she felt it necessary, without causing serious family conflict.

Not all the students were able to speak so positively about the changes which had taken place during the year. For some, the struggle and antagonism at home made the reality of being a student a stressful and problematic experience. Marilyn Smith was married to a lecturer in higher education, one of the few graduate husbands who managed to thwart his wife's coping strategies. He supported her academically by getting books for her from his institution's library and read through her essays. But on the eve of an examination when Marilyn wanted to revise, he did not give her the practical help she needed to work quietly in preparation for the next day. Instead, he made things worse:

MS The children were very good on the whole, but on the evening before the exam I asked my husband if he would put the children to bed because I wanted to revise and he is not very good at putting them to bed. He just yells and yells and yells and they ended up in tears so I had to go and see to them.

DD So it wasn't really any help to you?

MS In fact it was the reverse and it ended up taking twice as long to put them to bed and my youngest daughter woke up in the night before my first exam, so I hardly got any sleep. She always does this to me. Although he thinks he helps, he doesn't. I mean he's got quite a responsible job. He just sort of thinks that he should come home in the evening and he should relax and talk to me about his work.

There appeared to be scant negotiation between Marilyn and her husband with regard to childcare or housework. What little adaptation there was seemed to be on a piecemeal basis with no clear strategy or plan. The consequence for Marilyn was continual fatigue and a strong sense that she was not coping at any level. She felt conflict as a mother, frustration as a wife and exhaustion as a student. There was also little evidence of the achievement or exhilaration which many of the women said they felt at the end of the year. Despite academic ability, Marilyn struggled through the rest of the course and faced particular difficulties with teaching practice. Unhappily, she was the one student in the research group who failed her final teaching placement. She did not take up the opportunity given to her to repeat her school placement in the hope that she would pass the second time but instead withdrew from the course.

Explanations for Marilyn's regrettable outcome can only be speculated upon. Whether it was her husband's intransigence, her own inability to negotiate effective coping strategies or her possible unsuitability to teaching, is difficult to judge. What was clear was that, despite valiant efforts on her part, she was not able to forge coping strategies which reduced conflict in her family and the cumulative effects of this struggle led, not surprisingly, to emotional exhaustion.

Marilyn's case demonstrates the importance of a careful assessment about the time and circumstances for entering teaching which I discussed in Chapter 1. Central to this weighing up of the many factors which women with families have to consider is the need to involve the family in the details of changes which such a course of action will mean for them. There also has to be a recognition that as the course progresses, further changes will have to be robustly negotiated along the way with a clear focus on the goal and its subsequent benefits to everyone when it has been achieved.

When family conflicts looked likely to threaten the progress of some of the other mature women in the study, they succeeded in finding strategies which avoided conflict and cleared the way for them to continue their studies. In some cases this meant that the women did most of their work in the college library rather than at home and one woman worked in her local library on Saturday mornings. This allowed her to work efficiently without interruption, thereby freeing the rest of the day to spend with the family. In the severest case, the strain caused by frequent matrimonial disputes led to one woman separating and eventually divorcing her husband. The satisfaction and stimulation she was deriving from the course and her newly discovered academic and student identity became too important to give up so she built a new life for herself as a single parent and prospective teacher.

An examination of the women's coping strategies over the year showed that they were a dynamic and creative part of their adjustment to the student teacher role. They helped to illuminate the changes that were taking place within themselves and in the context of their family lives. These strategies were not uniform and differed according to the individual and her personal, familial and economic circumstances. Some women were undoubtedly better off than others, giving them access to a wider range of coping strategies. However, regardless of the differences in social and economic circumstances, most of the women succeeded in finding coping strategies which served their needs. Moreover, they highlighted some instances of indomitable human courage and resourcefulness in the face of some intractable and enduring problems.

It is to be hoped that the unswerving determination of these women to become teachers will inspire and encourage others to believe that such a goal is also possible for them.

Notes

1 Taken from Richardson, R. (1996) *Fortunes and Fables: Education for Hope in Troubled Times*. Stoke on Trent: Trentham Books, p.4. A compelling and sharply observant book which reaffirms the ideals, convictions and hopes which lead so many people into teaching, including the women whose stories provided the substance of this chapter.

2 As defined by *The Concise Oxford Dictionary of Current English*, 1990, Clarendon Press, Oxford.

3 Further details of this research can be found in Pollard, A. (1982) 'A Model of Classroom Coping Strategies', *British Journal of Sociology of Education*, 3, 1. pp.19-37.

4 Not all institutions of higher education have written examinations at the end of each academic year. Some depend solely upon course work for formal assessment, others have a mixture of on-going course assessment and written examinations. Whatever mode of assessment is adopted, an increasing percentage of marks count towards the final degree classification as the course progresses. Because so much hinges upon marks and grades, the outcome of essay and examination results is always a particularly exacting and stressful time for students.

5   The B.Ed degree classification system at this institution operated the following mark bands:

	Marks
1st	70-100
2.1	60-69
2.2	50-59
3rd	45-49
Pass	40-44
Fail	39-0

6   The seminar tutor for this particular programme. Because students had two sessions of the Primary Curriculum programme (a core foundation programme which introduced students to the Primary National Curriculum) each week, they saw more of this tutor than any other and s/he served as the student's personal tutor in the first year. However, in Pat's case, this tutor was not only her personal tutor but had also marked her essay.

7   In 1992 when Alan was made redundant, Britain was still in the grip of a severe recession. Several of the women in my study spoke of husbands who had lost their jobs, whose companies had gone into receivership, whose working hours were reduced or who lived under the daily threat of redundancy. Consequently, the financial circumstances of many women's families became very precarious during the four years of their training. By the end of the course at least 7 of the women were receiving social security benefits and many had to take out student loans in order to meet essential bills and running costs.

8   Most of the mature students used their tutorial appointments for the approval of essay plans so that they could check they were on the right lines before they began writing the essay. Not all students were as proactive as the mature women with many attending tutorials bereft of ideas or questions about reading in the hope that the tutor would provide them with ideas and suggestions about how to structure their essays.

9   Some of the advice on essay writing has been drawn from the excellent guide for students written by Winch, C. and Fairbain, G. (1991) pp. 34-35.

10 Many of the financial problems which beset the women during the years 1991-94 were a direct consequence of the economic recession which prevailed under both the Thatcher and Major Conservative governments. During this period, house prices soared leaving a growing trail of homeowners who experienced difficulty in paying their mortgages because of redundancy or reduced working hours. The point here is that whilst a four-year training course inevitably reduces the earning capacity of its students and brings with it a degree of financial stringency, the severity of some of the financial problems experienced by the women in the early 1990s, was exceptional and untypical.

11   Louise Woodward, a British nanny, was hired to care for the Eappen's eighteen month old baby son, Matthew, who died whilst he was in Woodward's care. Woodward was tried for murder in Boston, USA in 1997 and, after a lengthy, televised trial, convicted on a charge of murder. Subsequently, the judge's sentence of murder was reduced to one of manslaughter. The case later went to appeal in order to overturn the manslaughter charge but it was upheld.

12   Acker, S. (1980) 'Women, the Other Academics', in Equal Opportunities Commission, *Equal Opportunities in Higher Education*. Report of an EOC/SRHE Conference at Manchester Polytechnic, Manchester, EOC.

13   This quotation is taken from the writings of Coser, R.L. and Coser, L (1974) 'The Housewife and her Greedy Family,' in Coser, L. *Greedy Institutions: Patterns of Undivided Commitment*. New York: Free Press, cited in Edwards, 1993, pp 62-63.

Chapter 4

The experience of teaching

Imagine a sea of young faces looking expectantly at you as they wait for your first words of instruction. The children are seated on a carpet in front of you or at tables grouped around the room. You lay your carefully planned lesson notes to one side because you know you need to keep your eyes on the children if you are to hold their attention. You want to make your introduction to the lesson authoritative, interesting and appealing. Will they listen to me and do as I ask? What if I dry up in the middle of a sentence? Will they believe in me as their teacher? What will I do if they play up and refuse to cooperate? Will the ideas I have planned, work? These questions run through your mind at this eagerly awaited landmark in your training. The chance to put your ideas, beliefs and nascent teaching style into practice is what you've been waiting for. It has been the focus of your hopes and dreams and the culmination of several weeks' intensive preparation when much of what you have learned and read about should begin to make sense and fall into place. It is a defining moment. However, stunning or inept your first lesson may be, you get a real sense of whether or not you have the makings of a teacher. So what kind of training and help can you expect once you find yourself on a school placement and what is it like?

As part of a national drive to raise standards in teaching and pupils' achievements many changes have recently been made in the training of teachers. One important new initiative is the greater role which schools play in the teaching and assessment of trainees, particularly in the classroom-based elements of their training. The new model of training now rests on what is known as a *partnership* between higher education institutions and schools and this has become 'established as the main agent of delivery of effective training' (Teacher Training Agency, 1998, p.3).[1] What this means as far as you are concerned is that classteachers and school training mentors will play a prominent part in developing your repertoire of teaching skills and abilities. Depending on the model of partnership your particular training institution has adopted, university or college tutors will visit you in school on a specified number of occasions but your school-based training and assessment will be the *joint* responsibility of school personnel and your higher education institution. Although in some cases, you may find that this responsibility has shifted significantly towards the school. What used to be called 'teaching practice' has been replaced by 'substantial periods of work-based learning, along lines familiar to other professions, such as medicine and social work' (TTA, 1998, p.3). To ensure that the increased time which school staff have to spend working with student teachers, planning courses and attending training sessions at their partnership institution is appropriately resourced, a proportion of the money paid to training providers by the Teacher Training Agency has been transferred to schools. Schools and training institutions are regularly reviewed and monitored by Ofsted inspectors to check that the partnerships are providing effective and high quality training and that pupils, trainees and teachers are benefiting (TTA, 1998, p.11).

Partnerships vary in the way in which they organise patterns of teaching experience but, typically, you will have a mixture of day visits and several weeks' continuous experience, sometimes referred to as 'teaching blocks'. You can rest assured that you will not find yourself alone in the 'lion's den' without a fairly gentle and gradual build-up to the point where you are expected to take the whole class. Even then, the expectation will be that you will take the class for limited periods and for very focused and specific activities like taking the register or reading a story. As the course progresses you will receive training in the schools and at your college or university on how to teach all the subjects in the primary National Curriculum. Subject knowledge across ten areas takes time to build up so you will not be expected to assume the full range of classteacher responsibilities until you have gradually acquired the competences which allow you to do this with a measure of confidence. To begin with, you will work with small groups or individual children on specific tasks, often in the three core subjects – mathematics, English and science. In English, for example, you might be asked to hear a child read, noting what he or she can and cannot do in terms of reading performance or you could be asked to prepare a short group activity aimed to improve pupils' spelling or knowledge of letter sounds. In all probability, you will be asked to evaluate these sessions and give some indication of how they could be improved and what you might do next. The planning and evaluation of these first group sessions is likely to take place with peer group and tutor support as an integral part of your taught course. Partnership arrangements may also give you the opportunity to observe experienced teachers at work. Working in close contact with school subject co-ordinators will help to enhance your own subject knowledge and develop your understanding of how to make subject material appealing and accessible to children with diverse learning needs. You will also meet children from a variety social and of ethnic backgrounds, some of whom will be learning to speak English as an additional language and who may require specific language support.

An important part of your training in school and in higher education will be spent on helping you to implement the moral, ethical and educational principle of ensuring equality of opportunity for all the children in your care. This means that, from an early stage in your training, you need to be thinking about how you can find ways of ensuring that children with learning difficulties, behavioural problems, differing cultural and linguistic backgrounds have their needs met to succeed and achieve their educational potential. The opportunity to see how experienced and skilled classroom practitioners meet this challenge on a day-to-day basis is one of the many advantages of effective partnership arrangements.

In all probability, you will be attached to one or two schools each year within your chosen age range, although the timing of age-related placements may vary from one institution to another. Some institutions place their first years in schools according to their preferred age range from the start: others leave this until the second year in the belief that new trainees need experience of the entire primary age-range before they commit themselves to Key Stage One (infants) or Key Stage two (juniors). Whatever form of organisation you encounter, your first days in school will be spent observing children and teachers and getting to know the class before you are required to undertake the planning and teaching of small group activities.

So what do these first encounters in the classroom as student teachers feel like from the mature students' perspective? Do they live up to expectations? Is the gradual build-up to full classteacher responsibility a welcome relief or a frustrating constraint? The responses of the women in my research study revealed some intriguing and unexpected findings, especially in relation to their reception in schools, although it is important to bear in mind that the research on which these accounts are based took place just before partnership approaches to training began. Their experiences show powerfully that assumptions about teaching practice based on previous voluntary or paid classroom experience are best laid aside when the power relationship with the classsteacher shifts from 'helper' to student teacher. The other significant issue is that whilst there is now greater uniformity in schools in the curriculum and its assessment, wide variations remain between schools as far as ethos and staff-pupil interrelationships are concerned.

Welcome guests or 'spare parts'?

The first year placement for the women in the study came at the end of the year, after the written examinations. They had been attached to their respective schools since the Spring term and had been on several one or two-day visits so were reasonably familiar with the class and had generally begun to form a working relationship with the classteacher. It was a one week placement during which they were expected to work mainly with an identified group of children and assume some specific, whole class responsibilities. With the support of their college supervisor and classteacher, they were expected to demonstrate that they could plan lessons and teach them effectively within the context of a beginning student placement. The placement was assessed jointly by the classteacher and college supervisor and students had to pass before they could proceed to the second year. From the students' perspective, this was clearly a critical, final hurdle of the year.

The women often described their first teaching experience as 'the best moment of the course so far.' Most of their responses were charged with energy and animated intensity, as they recounted the work they had done with the children and how they related to the class teacher and the school as a whole. This early experience of the classroom served to confirm and justify the struggle many of them had been through to get on the course in the first place. Barbara Melling's ardent response to her placement was typical of several women in the group:

BM   I loved it in school. I really feel that's for me, you know. I was saying to my husband last night, I think I knew when I came to college, I knew exactly what my goals were and what I wanted and I don't think I'm going to change my mind. I just feel so relaxed. I feel, yes, I belong here. I feel I should be doing this so I've just got to work hard to get there but it'll be worth it.

The importance of feeling relaxed and belonging to the school as opposed to feeling an 'outsider', was signalled by Pat Grade in Chapter 2 as an important indicator of early adjustment to the academic demands of the course. A perception that they were accepted and at ease with themselves in school often made the difference between a confident or shaky beginning to the teaching practice. Linda Vince, for example, had spent several years working voluntarily in a primary school and felt strongly that her life experience as a mother facilitated the ease with which she related to the headteacher of a small, rural school.

LV   The headteacher had all the time in the world for us. She told me all about the school and all about her family. It was just two women talking together really. She made us feel very, very comfortable. They went out of their way to be helpful to us. She said she was thrilled to have us. I came away thinking, this is a dream school with everything working that she's trying to get working. I was very happy with the young age group even though it's not my preferred age group – but I was so tired!

The fact that Linda and her headteacher were both women with family responsibilities got their relationship off to a good start. Their experience of motherhood was mutually respected and helped Linda to feel that she could begin the process of developing a professional relationship from a position of shared understanding and life experience. It was, in her view, a significant factor in what proved to be a very successful and rewarding teaching experience.

Not all the mature students were so warmly welcomed and for some, their maturity and previous experience was considered irrelevant or ignored and they found their new role as student teachers restrictive and frustrating. Carole Payne, for instance, had enjoyed several years' teaching and organisational experience in the Red Cross. This work brought her into regular contact with schools and she was confident about her ability to communicate successfully with children and teachers. She was both surprised and disappointed with the marginality of her role in the classroom and said she felt like a 'spare part':

CP The one thing that's surprised me ... the one thing that I don't enjoy is the teaching practice and it's shocked me to the core because I love being with the children which is why I wanted to teach. But the jobs that I've done with the children up till now ... I always felt I could do more. I think I go in and I feel very much on the fringe and I can't be myself and I know I can't teach yet but I feel I know the children so that I feel ... I just can't explain it. I just come away thinking I just can't wait till I'm in my own position. I do feel a spare part and you have to wait to be asked to do something and I think we intimidate the teachers more than they intimidate us, perhaps. The mature students particularly, because they know that we're there to observe them and that must be awful. So I'm aware of that. ... I feel I won't ever learn what my style is until I teach. I find it very tedious, the "Could you work with this group?" I don't know what the children are capable of and all I do is supervise them which is boring.

The problem for Carole was that she already had considerable classroom experience. In her Red Cross work she frequently had to talk to whole classes of children and was used to holding her own in discussions, fielding questions and giving explanations. She had, not unreasonably, expected her school practice to pick up from the point she had left off as a Red Cross organiser. Instead, she became frustrated when all she was allowed to do was work with groups of children in a supervisory capacity. She could not engage in the more rewarding activity of teaching because she did not yet know the capabilities of the children, so what she had expected to be enjoyable and challenging, turned out to be disappointingly tedious and undemanding. It caused her to feel a certain amount of role strain[2] – she couldn't be herself, could not make use of the ability and skills gained in her earlier position and was 'shocked to the core' by her dislike of the first teaching placement.

Carole was not the only woman to experience this discomfort at being relatively marginalised in the classroom. Approximately one third of the group were disappointed and dissatisfied by their first school placements largely because their earlier work had been so much more satisfying. Many of them had earned respect in the schools they had worked in before and had been treated as though they were members of staff. Even when they did not have the same status as teachers, they often undertook similar responsibilities, putting up displays of children's work and supervising the class in the teacher's absence. Indeed, the work of these women was often so highly valued that it was the teachers and heads with whom they worked who had encouraged them to train as teachers in the first place. These contradictory and unexpected reactions to teaching experience caused the women considerable conflict. They could not and did not want to revert to their previous roles as parent-helpers or classroom assistants but found their new role as student teachers ambiguous and tenuous. This is compounded by an awareness that their classteacher might be uneasy about working with a student who had considerable classroom and life experience. Carole Payne was clearly sensitive to this possibility when she remarked, 'I think we intimidate the teachers more than they intimidate us perhaps.' So whilst students like Carole are keen to take on more responsibility and use the skills they have already acquired, they are constrained from so doing in case they are perceived by the classteachers as threatening. Related to this was the need to be wary of 'overstepping the mark', and encroaching upon the classteachers' domain of power and control, thus risking further problems in the delicate business of negotiating a working relationship with them.

Can anything be done to avoid such a problematic and anticlimactic experience? One problem lay with the timing and length of the placement: it was at the end of the summer term and only a week long Such a short period so late in the term probably militated against the forging of close working relationships which might have helped first year students. Secondly, one of the statements in the placement documentation sent to schools, indicated that first year students should be seen by teachers 'as another pair of hands' and schools interpreted this statement differently. Where the interpretation was prosaic, students found themselves being used more as classroom aides or parent-helpers than student teachers. In other schools, students who demonstrated confidence and teaching ability were given a freer rein and readily seized opportunities to take on more demanding teaching responsibilities. One of the constraints in the allocation of school placements is that so many factors have to be taken into account – proximity to the student's home, year-group preference, type of school and so on – that matching the school and class to the student's individual ability needs is almost an impossibility. So what school you end up in has more to do with luck than design. Whilst it is clear that some partnership schools have developed more effective structures and support systems than others, if you find yourself challenged by classteacher relationships and school organisation, you have to try and make the experience as positive as possible for your own teacher development. If, after giving it your best shot, you believe there are too many factors inhibiting your ability to succeed or make progress, then you have to discuss this openly with your college or university tutor, school mentor (where one exists), classteacher and headteacher. In cases of extreme difficulty, an alternative placement is sometimes the only solution, but you have to bear in mind that universities and colleges only have a finite number of schools in which they can place students.

One of the lessons to be learned is that regardless of how much experience and classroom confidence you feel you have, you are likely to avoid the worst effects of disappointment in your first teaching experience if you are prepared to be treated like a beginner, at least in the early days. It would seem to be in the nature of most new situations, be it a hospital, school or office, that the newest arrival has to work through a *rite de passage* before being accepted by the incumbents. Even after years of successful classroom practice, headship and a position as an education tutor in an institution of higher education, my diplomatic skills were taxed to the limit when I returned to the classroom for a term to update my primary teaching experience. It was some time before I was accepted by the classteacher with whom I was working and there were several occasions early on when I was firmly put in my place if I unwittingly stepped out of line. The power relationships between teachers and their respective classes are often finely balanced and painstakingly forged. Few self-respecting teachers will risk fracture to this relationship by the activities of a putative teacher until they are confident that their position or hard work with the class will not be threatened.

If you are lucky, your maturity, experience and ability will be warmly welcomed and quickly put to use; if not, hold on to the fact that for the most part, classteachers are human beings who need time to assess the kind of role they can play in helping you to develop as a teacher. During this time, behaviour which might initially strike you as cool and distant may be because you are being sized up for your potential to work successfully with both the classteacher and the children. Faced with what they perceive as overconfidence in their student teacher, classteachers might defend themselves by backing off, remaining aloof or actively seeking to find faults and flaws in your practice. Finding an acceptable balance somewhere between strident assuredness and timorous uncertainty is a matter of sensitivity and judgement founded upon experience and emotional intelligence.[3] Fortunately, the life and work experience of mature students often provides them with sharply alert antennae to this delicate negotiation and a significant factor in its success is the ability to sense the cues accurately, the subject of the next section.

Getting an accurate reading of the cues

Some of the mature women in my research found that their former jobs which involved work with different groups of people like nursing, caring for the elderly or social care work in a children's home, was especially helpful in sensitising them to the difficulties that teachers might face in having to work alongside a mature student who was of a similar age or older than themselves. They were particularly conscious of the discomfort that their presence might create for the teacher whom they were required to observe and this sometimes meant that they were more passive and deferential than they might have preferred. This was a conscious and deliberate strategy designed to help them build a relationship with the classteacher to gradually win their confidence in the long term. Beth Wells describes the dilemmas this created for her and the classteacher and how she succeeded in overcoming them through a series of adaptations, which resulted in a successfully negotiated relationship which worked for both parties:

BW My teacher ... um ... she was a bit perturbed by my being there and it took her a long time to sort of have a bit of confidence in me. It was difficult and I just feel that she hadn't a lot of confidence herself and she found it difficult having me there and she liked to sort of send me out of the room with a group which was fine but I could feel that she ... um ... she found it difficult and like at breaktimes, she would sort of disappear... So my teacher, I felt was difficult but by the end of the school experience we had a very good friendship. We'd both got children the same age and I think that's what she found difficult ... that we were a similar age and that we had children the same age. By the end of the time we were able to compare notes. She was able to give me lots and lots of information. She was able to say, "Well this lesson didn't go very well, did it?"

DD It sounds as though you did a lot of adapting on your part?

BW I think I did, really. But I do feel that I get on very well with most people and I don't sort of jump in. I do sort of study people and try and see how ... you know, I do feel that that's a skill I gained through working with older people and having to adapt to people.

Beth's teacher initially had to do what I described earlier, that is, to give herself the time and space she needed to work out the role she could play in helping Beth's professional development when she was the same age as herself and professionally capable. Because Beth had accurately sensed this need on her teacher's part, she bided her time, initially playing a passive, helping role in the classroom until her class-teacher felt able to take on a more authoritative and confident position as Beth's mentor and guide. As a result, Beth succeeded in learning a great deal from her classteacher and ended up by enjoying the practice.

I asked Christine, if she, like some mature students, had found the school experience restrictive and disappointing:

CK Oh no. Perhaps I just muscle in too much but I have plenty to do. I have a great time. I've found being a mature student a tremendous advantage because I'm able to communicate with the teachers so much better ... well, I think perhaps I do.

DD Some mature students have found the teachers backing off them a bit, perhaps because they are a bit threatened by them?

CK Yes, I think certainly. I try not to hang around as if I'm watching every move they make. I try to take myself to the other side of the classroom.

Christine's life and work experience along with her own reflexive ability had taught her that to move in too soon on another person's space can be irritating and stressful. She quickly saw that to 'hang around' too closely to the teacher in her observations and to ask her questions at every opportunity, would be against both her and the teacher's interest. So, far from 'muscling in', she kept a physical distance from the teacher and quietly engaged herself with a group of children. This gave the teacher the opportunity she needed to observe that Christine was a competent student and soon entrusted her with more demanding teaching responsibilities.

I subsequently labelled the strategy used by Beth Wells as '*strategic negotiation*' and that used by Christine Kift as *strategic distancing*'. The skills and sensibilities acquired in their previous employment helped them to achieve an accurate 'reading' of the classroom situation which was successful in both anticipating and dealing with potential difficulties between themselves and their respective classteachers.

In his study of newly qualified post-graduate teachers' entry into the teaching profession, Lacey[4] wrote that the ability to carry out a strategy successfully was dependent on the individual's ability to read the available cues accurately. In situations where individuals have to adjust to the norms of a new culture, particularly in institutions like schools, hospitals and prisons , newcomers have to learn the rules of the game. Part of an individual's ability to take part successfully in this 'game', whilst at the same protecting their individuality, is closely associated with whether or not they are able to 'read' people's behaviour in relation to themselves, the institution and other significant players within it. Some people appear to be cue-conscious and active cue-seekers whilst others are cue-deaf.[5] Both Beth and Christine were active cue seekers.

At the risk of over-simplifying what is in fact, a complex process of social change, your ability to develop as a teacher in relatively short bursts of time in the classroom will, to some, extent depend on your preparedness to pick up essential cues fairly quickly. The other 'layer' to this process of change is that these cues are not static; they change according to the context you are in at the time. In other words, different schools and classteachers will display their own particular cues whilst your ability to read them appropriately will improve with experience over a number of placements. What was clear from my research was that, for reasons already given, most mature students came to the course well equipped to read off cues from the behaviour of school personnel in ways which assisted their own position as student teachers. It may be that some people have greater cue-consciousness than others but the important thing is that you can make it easier for yourself to become a successful cue-seeker if you come to your first placement prepared to take account of perspectives other than your own. Being over-anxious or preoccupied with impressing the school with your experience and student-teacher prowess may impede your ability to cue-read accurately. On the other hand, if you use the skills and knowledge you have acquired in your work and life experience with the intention of understanding the classteacher's needs in relation to your own as well as finding ways in which you can best learn from her or him, you are more likely to gain positively from your first teaching placement.

Acquiring a student teacher identity

Believing in yourself as a student teacher is an important and defining moment in the journey towards qualified teacher status. It is different from the self-perceptions you may already have experienced in school settings. Once you begin to perceive that you and significant others believe in you as a student teacher, you will gain a palpable sense of what it will feel like to be teacher in your own right. When these feelings of teacher self-belief first begin to assert themselves, they are often accompanied by an uplifting and invigorating sense of achievement and personal change. All the work, uncertainty and hope in connection with your new career becomes vindicated. The fear always lurking at the back of your mind about whether this new addition to your 'self' would sit comfortably with the rest of your identity as a wife and mother, disappears at last.

So what has to happen before a student-teacher identity begins to take shape? Are there recognisable signs of change along the way? Does its emergence lie within your own control or that of others? I asked the women if they could articulate some of the changes and specify the factors which accounted for them.

For self-analysis of this kind, the women had to have an ability to step outside themselves to observe what was going on in their thinking and behaviour with respect to transitions in identity. In effect, I was asking the women to articulate the subtle changes which were taking place in the interaction between the instinctual, egocentric, 'I' and the more socially constructed 'me'.[6]

Most were able to offer surprisingly detailed and clear accounts of the shifts they felt they had made. The transition from their previous classroom identity as parent-helpers or paid assistants was partial for some and for others it was like quicksilver, fleeting and momentary. These women were experiencing glimpses of the changes that were taking place within themselves, but the student teacher role had not yet hardened into a firm or substantial identity. The transition involved the risk of losing the security and comfort of a known and certain role for another which was less certain and more problematic. Pat Grade, described how she constantly moved between the roles of parent-helper and student-teacher without feeling securely placed in either:

PG   I mean you go in and you're pretty much a dead fish, (sic) sort of thing. You're not one thing or another. You're not a parent-helper and I'm actually getting less responsibility than a parent-helper.

DD   So do you not feel that you're a trainee teacher yet?

PG   It's hard to say. I've been referred to as a trainee teacher and I've been referred to as a student. I feel that puts me down a lot. When I'm referred to as a trainee teacher, that's a lot better; it gives me a definition of the idea. But no, I still don't feel like a trainee teacher. I still feel like a parent. The teacher I'm working under is a lot younger than me and she only qualified two years ago and at times she keeps saying, "What do you think?" And I can't shift my role fast enough, do you know what I mean? I can't stand back and I can't be in it at the same time. I've got to be one thing or another.

Pat's reflexive and graphic account makes explicit the chimeric sense in which she still felt like a parent-helper, although her classteacher treated her as a student teacher, because there was a gap between the teacher's perception of her role and that which Pat had of herself. The classteacher's perception had jumped ahead of Pat's ability to see herself as a student teacher. The 'I' had not yet grasped the new 'me', which is arguably what Pat meant when she said, "I can't shift my role fast enough ... I can't stand back and I can't be in it at the same time."

The acquisition of a student teacher identity is dependent on a range of factors including the passage of time, self-knowledge, feedback from significant others and newly acquired skills and abilities. Knowing if and when this transition had occurred required a degree of self-consciousness and an ability to be self-analytical since the precise point at which change takes place between the 'I' and the 'me' is often elusive and difficult to define. However, whilst Pat was still unsure about whether she had moved away from her former identity as parent-helper at the end of her first year teaching practice, she was clear that she was making progress and could say what accounted for it:

PG   ... There's been a great shift in my thinking. The trouble is that when you go to into school you're at um ... a disequilibrium (sic) in yourself. You think to yourself, oh I'll just do that and that's what a parent-helper would do and there is already a parent-helper doing it ... and you think, oh where do I fit in now? It's sort of not one thing or another really. So I really had to stand back and take my cues from the teacher. I'd have to wait to be included because I wasn't really certain where to put myself.

DD How did you feel as the week progressed? Did you become clearer about your role?

PG Yes. As the week went on I became more confident in myself. I mean as a parent-helper, you have no control over anything, really, but as a trainee teacher you do have control. The teacher expects, if she goes out of the room to do something, that you won't let them climb all over the place. So there's a shift in power, really.

The progress which Pat had made by the end of the week's placement can be explained partly by the shifts she had made in her own thinking and partly by the expectations the teacher had placed on her to perform as a student teacher. Adapting to the role required a conscious decision to think herself into a new state of being. Pat had to think and act in ways which were markedly different from that of a parent-helper. An important point of progress for Pat was the teacher's expectation that she could keep control when alone in the classroom. She was charged with a responsibility which forced her to take up a more assertive and controlling role – which she described as 'a shift in power.' I later asked her what had helped her to feel that she was moving in the direction of believing in herself as a student teacher:

PG Um ... when they say to you, 'What do you think we should do?' Or being included in teachers' meetings, planning meetings and, 'Have you got any ideas on that?' And you think, right, yes, what I've got to say is important, you know. And they will actually act on it.

The ways in which the classteachers interacted with the women and the kind of responsibilities they gave to them were of central importance. Asking the students for their opinions and ideas made them feel they had a contribution to make and served to reinforce their status as student teachers. Pat felt that she still had some way to go before she could own to having a student teacher identity but she had made discernible progress, and her classteacher had contributed in much the same way that patients had done to student physicians' emergent identity as credible doctors, in Howard Becker's classic study of 1961 in which he documented the socialisation of medical students into qualified doctor status.[7]

Another important factor was the preparedness of the mature students to relinquish their previous auxiliary roles. A few initially opted for the relative safety of an ancillary role where they did not have to take the full responsibility for classroom control or for planning and resourcing lessons. Compared to the students who knew they had made a definite shift by the end of the week, they appeared less confident and more tentative about perceived changes in their identity. Brenda Corless, for example, was aware that she still had some way to go before she could believe in herself as a student teacher even though the classteacher had been very helpful to her in terms of treating her as one:

> BC I still think I've got another step to go, to be quite honest. I've always, like you say, been a helper and always been behind someone else ... so to take that step out, I felt very conscious of that. About Thursday or Friday, I thought, oh yes, I can handle this. They're (the children) taking notice of me ... but ... I don't think I've got there yet.

There would seem to be two indispensable conditions for progress towards a student teacher identity: the women's preparedness to shed former auxiliary roles in the classroom and the willingness of the classteacher to communicate to the students a clear and unambiguous view of themselves as student teachers and give them classroom tasks commensurate with the status of trainee teacher. This included taking the students into their confidence about children's needs and problems; referring to them in the children's presence as teachers rather than students; making a clear distinction between them and parent-helpers and inviting students to contribute ideas to meetings and future lesson planning.

The behaviour of other classroom personnel towards them was also significant, particularly the parent-helpers and classroom assistants. How the lower status school staff interacted with them was seen as an important reference point for their developing student teacher identity. If, for example, parent-helpers deferred to them during classroom encounters and classteachers manifested differential treatment of parent-helpers in the women's favour, the students saw this as a kind of 'marker' which indicated that they had succeeded in acquiring student teacher status.

Not surprisingly, what really mattered to the women was how pupils accepted their authority. If children were behaving as though they had accepted the student as their 'teacher' and this concurred with the view of the classteacher and college or university supervisor, the student had almost certainly begun to acquire a positive student teacher identity. Ann Major pinpointed the way she had dealt with an infant child's challenge to her status as a 'teacher' as concrete evidence that she acquired a student teacher identity:

AM I think it particularly happened in that week block and it happened particularly in one of the writing sessions ... and one of the children, quite a bright child, writes his name with a capital letter at the end of this surname and I said, 'You don't do that.' And he said, 'My Mum does it that way,' and I said, 'But you're at school now and we do it the right way at school.' And he said, 'But my teacher let me,' and I said, 'But I'm you're teacher this week and I'm not going to let you because I want it done properly.' And he did, and he did it correctly the whole week and I think if there was a moment, then that was it.

The child's challenge provided Ann with an important test. She was not de-railed by his reluctance to do what she asked and when he eventually complied, it served to confirm her student teacher identity.

Roughly half the women in the study felt that they had achieved a student teacher identity by the end of their first year and others were moving towards it. But for even the most confident and secure students, their student teacher identity was not necessarily a stable perception at this point in their training. Differing contexts and relationships between school staff, pupils and education tutors could temporarily destabilise the tenuous hold on that emergent student teacher identity. However, as the women increased in skill, knowledge and confidence over the years so the fluctuation decreased.

What I have been trying to signal throughout this discussion is that acquiring a student teacher identity can be rather like trying to catch a moonbeam in the early weeks. 'First you have it, now you don't ,' is often how it feels. Its acquisition is influenced by both yours and the classteacher's response to the situation. Equally important is the changing nature of the social relationship between yourselves, the pupils, classteacher and college or university tutor. Sometimes progress may be inhibited by your own reluctance to take on the weight of responsibility demanded of putative teachers. On other occasions, it seems that no matter how hard you try, barriers are erected each time you try to become the 'teacher'. This may be because the classteacher is reluctant to pass over her/his authority to you or because there are so many inherent difficulties in the organisation and composition of the class that you are impeded by the complexity of its arrangements or its problems with behaviour management. Perhaps the most disheartening of experiences occur when for one reason or another, the relationship between yourself and the classteacher is not conducive to your progress and development as a teacher or, worse still, when a precarious student/ teacher relationship undermines your fragile confidence. The wise and sensitive counsel of an experienced secure mentor is of paramount importance in helping you to keep a sense of proportion. If you can satisfy yourself that you have done all you can to be consistently pro-fessional in your dealings with children and staff and that you are meet-ing the planning, teaching and assessment requirements of the practice, your abilities will be recognised, regardless of the frustrations brought about by the context of the placement.

There are such wide discrepancies between school and classroom contexts and the relationships of the human beings within them are so complex that it can be impossible to be sure whether the cause of the problem lies with the student, the class, the classteacher, the school itself or a combination of all these factors. Over many years of student supervision – and many of my education colleagues would report similarly – it is not unusual to see the same student fare disastrously in one school and outstandingly well in another.

On the positive side, however complex and problematic teaching ex-perience can be, it is usually a time of immense professional growth and intense satisfaction. Mature students are generally warmly welcomed by school staff and their abilities, experience and maturity swiftly har-nessed in the joint interests of theirs and the children's educational bene-fit.

The now consolidated partnership arrangements between schools and training institutions have also sharpened and enhanced the training skills of classroom teachers and school mentors. Most classroom teachers take their training responsibilities seriously and do their best to anticipate the problems encountered by student teachers before they become major obstacles to progress. For the most part, the partnership which now exists between schools and training institutions has worked to the trainee's professional advantage and there are undoubted gains for the schools and most importantly, for the pupils themselves, but human beings are complex and schools are no less so. It would be surprising therefore if school experience were not without its share of flaws, disappointments and difficulties in even the most meticulously forged partnership system.

Notes

1   Teacher Training Agency (1998) *The Use of Resources in Partnership: A Working Paper.* London: TTA.

2   The term 'role strain' has been used in sociological research to conceptualise the tension and conflict felt by an individual when there is a mismatch between one set of cultural role expectations and another. For example, research on entry into teaching by Becker (1952) and Whiteside *et al.*, (1969) found that newly qualified teachers were often acutely surprised by the difference between the view of pupils presented by their training institutions and that of the more punishment-centred culture of schools. Because the difference between the two cultures was so marked, its impact on individuals was described as 'reality shock'. The full references for this research can be found in the bibliography.

3   Goleman, D. (1996) *Emotional Intelligence; Why it Matters More than IQ.* London: Bloomsbury.

4   Lacey, C. (1977) *The Socialization of Teachers.* Series: Contemporary Sociology of The School. London: Methuen.

5   The concept of 'cue-consciousness' originated from the work of Miller and Partlett (1974) *Up to the Mark.* London: Society for Research into Higher Education.

6   The theory underpinning the understandings which can be learned from 'I – me' interactions, is taken from a branch of social psychology known as '*symbolic interactionism*' . In 1902, Cooley argued that through our interactions with other people we learn to see ourselves as we think others see us. Mead (1934) later expanded upon this idea, claiming that 'the 'I' (ego) can observe, be aware of and think about 'me' (alter).' In other words, we experience ourselves in the same way that we experience other people. The 'self' is therefore fundamentally social.

7   Becker, H.S., Geer, B., Hughes, E.C. and Strauss, A.L. (1961) *Boys in White. Student Culture in Medical School.* Chicago: University Press.

Chapter 5

Getting a job

You are now within sight of qualified teacher status. All your teaching practices are successfully completed and you know enough about the National Curriculum and the management of pupils to take on the responsibility of a class of your own as a beginning teacher. In the early part of the Spring term of your final year, you will need to begin the process of job application and interview preparation. Some of this preparation will form part of the final programme of your education course along with training and updating in contemporary classroom issues.

The business of getting a job is exacting and time consuming when you are trying to complete dissertations, course assignments and prepare for final examinations. In many ways it couldn't happen at a more pressured time when you are working at full stretch to ensure that you accumulate all the assessed marks you need for the final degree classification which you feel your course work profile merits and deserves. You therefore need to be very well organised in your final year so that you can give this important task the time and energy it will inevitably soak up.

The purpose of this chapter is to set out what is involved in the different stages of job application and to offer some practical advice on how best to market yourself. I wanted to ensure that I was drawing upon fresh insights so I recently re-interviewed some of the women in my original research study, most of whom have now been in full-time teaching posts for at least three years, and asked them to recollect their experiences of job applications and interviews. They were applying for their first teaching posts in 1995, a difficult time in the teacher job market for reasons which will become clear. Many of the things they shared with me about what makes a strong or bland letter of application, how best to prepare for interviews and how to deal with disappointment and rejection, are rich in learning potential.

Schools are now much more demanding and prescriptive in their job advertisements than they were some ten to fifteen years ago. Gone are the days when applying for a teaching post required little more than the completion of an application form and a fairly informal letter of application in the hope that you would be invited to a friendly interview which, having achieved, you might have thought about the night before. Gone too are the times when it was considered reasonable to assume that, provided you presented yourself as a good classroom practitioner with one or two curriculum interests which you were prepared to contribute to the life of the school, you would, have stood a credible chance of being appointed. Staffing needs now have to be tied in closely with the school development plan as well as any action plans arising from recent Ofsted reports. Given the central importance of staffing decisions, new appointments can no longer be left to the individual whim of a headteacher but are now more properly the province of wider discussions between senior management teams, school governors and parent representatives.

Within this context many advertised teaching posts now set out to attract applicants who will satisfy a particular need or fill a specific gap in the school's teaching profile, so a particular subject specialism is likely to figure prominently in the advert. You will be given advice about where to find lists of teaching vacancies from your institution's careers advice centre. Some will be in the form of Local Authority pools where you submit a general application for consideration by a Local Authority panel which will, if you are successful, direct you to any one of a number of teaching vacancies. Others will take the form of individual school advertisements in the appointments pages of the educational press like the *Times Educational Supplement* or the Education sections of *The Guardian* or *The Independent*. Vacancies are also listed in Local Authority bulletins which are circulated to schools and sometimes to university or college careers departments. There are also the informal networks which operate by word of mouth or insider information as is the case when a student who has done particularly well on a school placement, may be invited to apply for a forthcoming vacancy with the strong possibility that they will be offered the post. Schools are often keen to appoint newly qualified teachers who are known quantities and can offer the strengths and skills they need.

What is involved in applying for a first teaching post?

Whilst the details of application and interview requirements vary from school to school, you need to be prepared to give considerable thought and time to this labour intensive task In addition to a completed standard application form, most schools now expect to receive a well-presented curriculum vitae and a letter of application. It is important that you read the small print on the application form carefully because some schools and Local Authorities specifically request that you send *not* a separate letter of application but a succinct personal statement in support of your application. Indeed, the ability to select and write succinctly about what you consider to be the salient supporting information, may be part of the selection criteria. The interview itself often involves three distinct parts: the candidate's response to a range of questions put by an interview panel which is likely to include the head-teacher, a senior member of staff, one or two members of the school governing body who may be a parent and/or a teacher governor; a portfolio of teaching evidence and a presentation. Interviews also vary quite considerably in length; some schools require candidates for half a day, others a whole day and more rarely, as much as two days. The interview and its constituent parts will be discussed further on in the chapter. For now, one of the first things which you will be concerned about is where and what jobs you should apply for.

Where to apply

For mature students this consideration frequently boils down to domestic pragmatics. Family considerations such as the children's schooling and their husband's or partner's employment usually mean they have to restrict their applications to schools which lie within a reasonable travelling distance from home. You have to decide how long a journey you can tolerate at the beginning and end of each day. But the mature student research group and students I am teaching currently, agree that a journey which exceeds forty-five minutes is too far to travel ten times a week. It would add at least an hour and a half to your day and longer when driving conditions are hazardous. You will also have learned from your teaching experiences that you need to be at school by 8.15am at the latest if you are to have everything prepared for the start of the day, and many teachers arrive considerably earlier. The school day is also periodically lengthened by staff meetings, training sessions and parent evenings. The latter can finish as late as 10pm and governors' meetings, if you elect to be involved, can finish even later. You therefore need to be realistic about the maximum length of time you can comfortably cope within an inherently demanding first year of teaching. The cumulative effects of travel fatigue can also make the difference between enjoying your work and tolerating it. And the longer the journey, the more it will cost in petrol or fares. Many of the women in my study had taken out at least two financial loans by the end of their training, especially those who were lone parents. They could ill afford to lose substantial sums of money from their first pay cheques on petrol costs whilst trying to repay loans, so schools outside a reasonable travel radius were out of the question.

Choosing the 'right' school

Finding a first post in a school in which you feel able to give of your best and which will nurture your development as a teacher is clearly of paramount importance. Feeling sure that the school which offers you a position is the right place for you to begin your career is often a matter of intution and the 'feel good' factor. I have often heard students saying about their job success: 'I knew the school was right for me the moment I got there'. But intutition or 'gut instinct' is not entirely based on raw emotion; it is frequently influenced by the way school personnel approach you and how welcome they make you feel. More importantly, what they have to say about their beliefs and value systems with respect to children and learning also feed into the mental data you have assimilated about the school. This is why it is a good idea to visit the school before the interview so that you can make your decision to accept the job or not on the basis of as much information as possible. Given that accepting any new job or opportunity inevitably involves a certain amount of risk, you need to be as certain as you can be that your first teaching post is in a school where you will be happy and likely to develop as a new teacher.

However, in recognising the significance of this important step in your teaching career, the title of this section is misleading because it presumes that you have relative freedom over the choice of your first school when in fact, your ability to control the application process is heavily constrained. For example, constraints about where you can apply are factored into the equation from the outset. In addition, you are limited to those posts which fall within the compass of your training, particularly with respect to Key Stage expertise and subject specialism. So is the whole process outside your control leaving you no role but the fate of happenstance? No, it isn't. Despite the inbuilt constraints of market competition, distance and the school's own agenda, you do have some control over the process. This lies firstly with the decisions you make about how to present yourself in a letter of application.

Selling yourself: the letter of application

Your first introduction to a potential headteacher comes in the form of paperwork – your application. This document sends a very strong signal about the kind of professional you are, how much you value yourself and how much effort you have invested in communicating clearly why you believe you are a strong candidate for the post. Your application form needs to be professionally presented, legible and with due attention paid to spelling and grammar. Despite the career significance which hangs on this I continue to hear about applications which are poorly presented and peppered with mistakes and deletions. Applications of this kind waste everyone's time and inevitably end up in the reject pile. If you are serious about wanting the post, it is worth spending time to make it look good and read well. It could, after all, be the passport to several rewarding years in your first teaching post. The content of your letter has also to engage and interest the reader and to promote you in a way which helps to differentiate you from the rest of the candidates.

Students often start out by assuming that writing a letter after years of writing essays and lesson critiques will be relatively easy until their first three or four attempts end up in the waste basket! Writing about yourself in a positive and upbeat way without sounding overly self-conscious, insincere or like 'Goody Two-Shoes', demands an ability to write simply, clearly and directly about the knowledge and expertise you possess. It is, in fact, a demanding and painstaking task. Because training programmes are now so crammed with subject knowledge and preparation in the latest Government initiatives, you are likely only to receive rather general guidance about what should be included in a letter of application. Indeed, the mature students I recently spoke to bemoaned the lack of help they received at college unless they were fortunate enough to find a tutor who knew them well and was prepared to go through their letter in some detail. At some years' distance from the experience, they were able to say what they thought were the important elements in a successful letter of application. In the following extract, Christine Kift explains why she now thought that her first letter of application did not display her many qualities in the best light:

CK ... And when I look at it now, I actually called it up on the computer and I cringed because if I was recruiting someone, what I said in my letter and what I was told to say in my letter (by the college), was not really what I want to know because it was devoid of personality. It was like a list: I can do this, I have done that and it didn't really say an awful lot about me as a person and I think this is where the job I got, I got because I went in with a big smile – 'Hello. Here I am. This is me and this is what I'm like. Would you like to look at my CV?' I think if Peter (her current headteacher) had seen the letter, he would have filed it and thought, Yes. Ok, but nothing special. I think the next time I apply for a job the letter itself will be shorter and more about what I am, who I am and what I think rather than just a list of things.

Christine makes some very helpful points, particularly about the need for the letter to communicate a strong sense of who you are and what your teaching beliefs and priorities are. Important, too, is the need to err on the side of crisp conciseness rather than laborious detail. There are three main qualities which you need to provide in the letter: presentation, content and the specifications of the teaching advertisement. The following principles and guidance should help your thinking when you are ready to write.

Writing the letter of application

- The main objective is to achieve an interview. Keep this at the forefront of your mind.

- Try not to repeat what is written elsewhere in your CV, application form or professional reference from your college or university. This will free you to write about what interests and motivates you as a person and beginning teacher.

- The letter should include supporting information which sells you as a person with respect to your individual beliefs and priorities about teaching and learning. Make it interesting to read and keep your readers in mind all the time you write (head, governors and parents).

- Avoid the temptation to write down everything you know about yourself. Write enough to whet the appetite of a future employer leaving scope to elaborate in greater detail at the interview.

- Aim for a maximum of two word-processed sides of A4.

Presentation

- The completed product should convey high professional standards and signal that you are a serious candidate who has thought very carefully about the content of your application.

- Word process your letter on good quality paper using one side only.

- When you have selected a final draft for copying, take it to be proof-read by a friend or someone whose written English skills are very secure. Get your application form checked at the same time. Spelling and grammatical accuracy really matters as does correct punctuation. A careless error on the first page of your form or letter could mean that you are out of the race before you get to the first hurdle. Leave yourself *ample* time for the meticulous checking and excising of errors.

Content

- Write in simple, clearly expressed English and avoid jargon.

- Aim to communicate what it is that is special and interesting about your particular approach to teaching and learning including your preferred methods of classroom organisation.

- Write honestly about your strengths and professional qualities. Avoid the temptation to inflate your abilities or indicate that you are prepared to do almost anything extra which the school demands. The former will make you sound unconvincing and the latter, desperate.

- Include a paragraph about your subject specialisms stating what you believe is worthwhile and exciting about them. Give one or two examples of particular teaching successes which demonstrate your confidence in subject knowledge and your commitment to stimulating pupils' interest in their content.

- Make one or two points about your reaction to a recent Government initiative indicating what your teaching priorities might be. If you are writing about the literacy hour, for example, you might wish to emphasise the stress you would place on drama as a way of improving and enriching literacy skills.

- Acknowledge areas you are keen to work at and develop but avoid baring your soul and listing all your weaknesses.

- Be positive and clear about the advantages you can offer as a mature student. Your maturity, wisdom and life experience should be a strong feature of your application.

- Finish by indicating why you are interested in this particular post. Communicate what it was that attracted you to it and refer to favourable features of a visit you might have made before deciding to apply. Potential employers are likely to warm to candidates who have taken the trouble to find out about the special features of their school.

- Your final sentence is important. Try and find a form of wording which avoids either the obsequious or the triumphalist. If all else fails, aim for a straightforward, businesslike ending.

The advertised specifications of the post

- Once you have constructed your first satisfactory letter of application you can use it as a basis for other applications. However, it is most important that you adapt your letter to suit the requirements of the advertised post.

- It is important that your letter signals that you want *their* particular job, not simply *a* job.

- Communicate a clear sense in your letter that you have read and thought carefully about the additional details and requirements of the post which will have accompanied the application form.

- Show how your teaching profile and particular strengths fit the requirements of the job specification.

Selling yourself: the interview

The two issues about the interview process which the women in the follow-up study found most difficult to deal with were the diversity of practice in schools and the feeling that they had very little control over the method or outcome of the interview. When they were looking for their first posts in 1994, schools were just beginning to feel the see-saw effects of formula funding, in which some schools could end up with capital to spare whilst others found themselves faced with a budgetary deficit. Where primary schools had sufficient funds for the appointment of a new full-time member of staff, they were seldom able to offer a permanent contract until they knew for sure that their next annual budget was able to sustain a further full-time teaching salary. In this uncertain financial climate, one-term and one-year contracts became commonplace in the mid-1990s. The devolvement of financial control away from Local Education Authorities to schools also meant that heads and governors had increased powers with respect to teaching appointments. Formerly, schools had largely relied upon Local Authority pools from which they could select their first appointments and whilst some LEAs continued to offer a reduced pool service, schools were now free to advertise and interview independently of LEA involvement. However, some of the experiences of the mature women follow-up group showed clearly that this was new territory to schools with many still at 'first base' on the interview procedure learning curve. Karen James, for example, having waited several months for her first interview, was very disappointed by the way in which candidates appeared to be tolerated rather than welcomed in the school to which she had applied:

KJ   I was disappointed about the actual interview because I just felt it was a strange interview. They sat us in the staffroom and they were in and out the whole time making themselves drinks and things. We never got one and we were there forever. We never got a tour of the school which I thought was pathetic and when I went in (for the interview), I can't remember if it was random or alphabetical or what now, there must have been about five or six of us and we all had to wait for everybody else which I think is really silly. ... Quite a few of us felt it was really a strange interview and we didn't like it at all and coming away from that, I felt very cross and disappointed but in a strange sort of way, relieved as well because I felt if you are going to treat people like that, I don't really want to work there.

The school may have been under pressure which might have explained the 'strange' interview but its impact upon her created an unfavourable impression of the school and left her feeling despondent about her chances of success for several weeks afterwards. Although Karen had to settle for supply teaching for a couple of terms, she did eventually get a full-time post in a junior school.

Another difficulty for the women was the ambiguity which schools sometimes created between informal and formal interviews. The former usually gives the candidates an opportunity to look round the school and learn more about the expectations of the post whilst one or two members of staff, usually the head and a senior member of staff, find out if they have the necessary experience for the job through informal conversation. In many ways, so-called informal interviews are more problematic than formal interviews because it is less clear what is expected of candidates. In the formal interview, you can at least expect an interview to be conducted by a panel of school-related staff in which you will be asked questions in connection with the advertised post. If you are invited to an event labelled 'informal interview', it is wise to assume that this could be as crucial to your chances of getting the post as the formal interview. However friendly staff appear to be whilst touring the school with you, their real purpose is to size you up in order to see whether you are what they are looking for. In these circumstances the questions *you* ask are as important as the answers you give. However, in some cases, often depending on the school's agenda and the availability of candidates, the informal interview can become the formal interview. The problem is that you may not be aware of this until the interview is over, or at least half way through. This can be a nerve-wracking experience for students new to the mysteries of interviewing practices, as two women in the study discovered. Linda Vince was invited to an 'informal meeting' but when she had been shown round the school she was asked very probing questions about the school's learning environment and what her impressions of the school were. She obviously answered well and gave a good account of her abilities because she was offered the post. In Pamela Jones's case the school invited potential candidates to telephone the school in order to make an arrangement to visit the school prior to a possible interview. When Pamela turned up for what she had anticipated would be a tour of the school, she found herself being interviewed. This had the effect of putting her on her back foot since this was not what she had prepared herself for and she did not get offered the post. Whilst these experiences would not be considered by many heads or school inspectors to be exemplary interview practice, I mention these examples here because it is not an uncommon experience for nervous candidates to discover that their expectations of what is meant by an interview do not necessarily match those of the school.

There are two points to be learned from these experiences: firstly, it is always in your interest to visit the school if invited to do so; if not, telephone and ask if one can be arranged. This will help you to focus your interview preparation and confirm whether or not you wish to proceed with your application. Be prepared for the possibility that your visit may develop into an interview. Secondly, do not read 'friendly and relaxed' into the term, 'informal' interview. Whatever guise it takes, it generally forms an important part of the assessment process and many hapless candidates have unwittingly talked themselves out of the job by engaging in a garrulous account of the difficulties they had in finding the school or telling a potential employer the story of their life. In such circumstances you need to be alert, focused, interested and intelligently responsive to all that you see and hear as well as constantly aware that you are being judged as a potential member of the school's staff.

Some years down the line of budgetary control and institutional management, schools are now more experienced at staff recruitment. Forever conscious of the need to spend wisely and to act in the interests of the school's medium and longer terms requirements, new appointment interviews are, on the whole, professionally managed and administered but much more demanding of candidates. In addition to the interview, schools now often request candidates to prepare a presentation on a specified topic and to present a portfolio of work. From the student's perspective this is a substantial additional burden at a time of intense coursework pressure. On the other hand, the presentation and portfolio requirements give you a good opportunity to demonstrate your teaching abilities, priorities and commitment. During these parts of the interview process, the stage is yours and, handled confidently, this is one area where you can take the reins and gain some control over what you want the interview panel to know and hear about you. So think positively and seize the chance to sell yourself. Once you have got a presentation and portfolio prepared to your satisfaction, they can be used or adapted for other interviews.

The guidance offered below sets out some basic advice on each of the three aspects of the interview which other students have found reassuring and helpful. It is based on the recent training experiences of both B.Ed and PGCE student teachers as well as insights gleaned from the mature student study.

Preparing for interview

- The single most important thing to hold steadfastly in mind both in preparation for, and during the interview, is a quiet, confident belief in your ability as a beginning teacher. Remember that you have passed each of your teaching practices because you have convinced classteachers, headteachers and education tutors of your potential to succeed as a qualified teacher. You have also undergone a rigorous and demanding training course which has prepared you well for this moment.

- Aim for a performance which is true to yourself and which communicates a sincere wish on your part to engage intelligently and thoughtfully with your interviewers. Remember that they, too, are human beings who may well find the business of asking questions as stressful and nerve-wracking as you do when answering them.

- Get hold of a list of current, frequently asked interview questions (your college, university or careers advisory service should be able to help with this) and practice asking and answering questions with a partner or small group of friends. Be critical friends for one another and give constructive feedback on how the questions were answered.

- Small group role-play scenarios where students take on the part of say, a headteacher, parent-governor and candidate in an interview simulation can be extremely valuable preparation, provided that it takes place in a non-threatening and supportive environment. It helps to have a specific job advertisement brief to focus upon.

- Be prepared to answer questions on contemporary classroom concerns, like the numeracy and literacy hours, for example. It is useful to think about them in terms of their relative advantages and disadvantages to teachers and children.

- Candidates are often asked what they think their relative strengths and weaknesses are. Answer this with reference to your teaching profile and think about so-called 'weaknesses' in terms of curriculum or organisational areas, for example, which you believe need further development. Remember too, that areas for development will change as you progress through your career – i.e. they are dynamic, not static and an effective teacher is *always* changing and developing.

- Opening questions designed to 'warm you up' and get you talking often focus on aspects of your teaching which you would describe as particularly successful or enjoyable. It helps to have some examples of your teaching successes clearly worked out in advance so you are not struggling to recall them from memory at the interview. Aim for a succinct, punchy response in which you indicate why you thought you were successful.

- Be similarly prepared for questions which focus on those aspects of your training you have most enjoyed or found most valuable.

- Think too about what your expectations of the school might be in terms of your own professional development as well as any plans you have for your longer term career aspirations.

- Visit the school in advance, if possible, and find out as much as you can about its priorities and immediate and longer term aims.

- Listen carefully to interviewers' questions and give yourself time to respond thoughtfully. If you have not understood the question do not be afraid to ask for clarification.

- Be prepared to acknowledge the complexities of some classroom problems and issues. No one has all the answers. In the case of difficult questions be open about the fact that your current views and thoughts are based on your limited experience so far and that these may change in the light of further experience.

Dress

- Aim for a professional, uncluttered appearance.

- Select clothes which are comfortable to wear and which make you feel and look good.

- Avoid wearing clothes which are too tight. Interview nerves are bad enough without adding discomfort with uncomfortable clothes.

- If it will boost your confidence to buy a new outfit especially for the interview: try to buy it well in advance so that you can get used to wearing it or have time to decide to discard it in favour of an alternative.

The Presentation

This can take the form of a talk on a particular aspect of teaching or a lesson which you teach to a group or class of children. In either case, your audience will usually be a small group comprising the head-teacher, a classteacher and one or two school governors. There are no hard and fast rules about the length of time you will be expected to talk or teach – it can be somewhere between five and forty-five minutes.

From the school's perspective, the key purpose of the presentation is to assess your communicative and teaching ability in comparison with other candidates. From your perspective, it gives you an opportunity to demonstrate your professional skills in action. You may be given a specific brief to talk about or prepare a lesson on, or you may be given the freedom to select a subject area or educational issue of your own choosing.

- If you are given a specific brief to talk on, make sure you stick to the point and keep strictly to the allocated time limit. Practice your talk with a respected friend whose opinions you trust and get him/her to comment honestly on your delivery and content as well as on your timing.

- If you are asked to teach a lesson there are strong, pragmatic and professional grounds for using material, resources and ideas which have worked well for you in the past. There is no need to reinvent the wheel.

- If you are not able to choose the aspect or theme of your lesson, you should still be able to draw upon material you have already used which you can then adapt to suit the presentation requirements.

- Try, wherever possible to use material you have considerable experience and knowledge of. Even better, if you can select material about which you feel enthusiastic and confident; this will communicate to your advantage during the presentation and will help you to feel more sure of your ground.

- Whether your audience is predominantly adults or children, try to engage in direct eye contact from time to time but avoid forcing it. Try to keep your behaviour as natural as the 'unnatural' circumstances of the presentation will allow.

- You are bound to feel nervous both before and during the presentation but remind yourself that in many respects, this ordeal is no worse than being observed and assessed by classteachers, education tutors or external examiners. You have had plenty of practice at performing in front of others and have clearly been successful at it or you would not have come this far.

- If you are teaching a lesson, provide enough copies of your lesson plan for your observers. It also helps your audience to know where you are coming from if you briefly contextualise your lesson by saying where it fits in with your medium term plan.

- If you are giving a talk, avoid the temptation to overwhelm your audience with material; only give them what is absolutely necessary for them to be able to follow your line of argument. If you are talking about an aspect of teaching, the inclusion of a lesson plan, one or two examples of children's work and an overhead transparency, for example, should be sufficient. Make sure all your materials are professionally presented and thoroughly scrutinised beforehand for errors. Overhead transparencies are better word-processed in an enlarged font but, if it is not already indicated on the interview briefing sheet, check first that your school possesses an overhead projector.

The presentation provides you with a ready-made opportunity to sell your teaching and communicative skills by using some of your best, tried and tested material. You have also had plenty of practice at giving them throughout the four years of your training so you are more than capable of giving a strong and assured performance. Go ahead and seize the day!

The portfolio

This presents you with an opportunity to share with the interview panel some of the highlights of your teaching experience which might, for example, include samples of children's work, lesson plans, lesson evaluations, schemes of work, reports on children's progress, photographs of classroom displays and observation comments from teachers and tutors.

Last year a number of the students I taught were asked to bring portfolios of work with them to the interview. This was a relatively new interview requirement and, initially, there was some anxiety about how they should set about this task and what the portfolio should include. In the end we decided that a focused and carefully selected range of items based on some of the above examples, which the student could then talk to, was the most appropriate strategy. The advice set out below is based on guidelines which have worked well for students in the past.

- Choose a limited number of teaching evidence examples which, taken together, form a coherent whole or theme. You might, for example, take a particular teaching and learning problem which you resolved by adopting a specific approach or by following particular teaching strategies.

- Aim to tell a teaching and learning story through your selection of teaching evidence examples.

- Don't shrink from acknowledging difficulties and problems which you experienced on the way. It will bring your 'story' to life as well as make it more interesting and real.

- Present your materials attractively in a folder which can be easily passed round.

You are not likely to have more than five to fifteen minutes to talk to your portfolio so six to eight items will be more than enough. Too many items and you will spend time leafing through your selection to find the page you want with the consequence that you risk losing the attention of your audience.

From the beginning of the 1998-99 academic year student teachers build up their own teacher education profiles from the first year onwards. These are substantial documents which will provide a detailed picture of students' progress and development across their academic and professional training. Students are able to select evidence to use at a first post interview and continue to update them throughout their teaching career.

Coping with rejection

When you have set your sights on a particular post, believed that you met the requirements of the job advertisement and prepared well for the interview, it is very disappointing to hear that someone else has been offered the position. Often, the first reaction is to speculate on where you might have gone wrong and which questions you did not answer to the panel's satisfaction. If you have not been appointed as a result of one of your first interviews, the chances are that it was less to do with any shortcomings in your performance and more to do with the fact that the chosen candidate had a particular combination of abilities, experience and curriculum strengths which better matched the school's requirements. Most schools these days offer an interview debriefing to candidates and you can often gauge from this whether it was your performance which let you down or whether someone else fitted the school's needs more precisely than your profile. If you are not offered a debriefing and you are unsure of the reasons why you were not selected, it is worth contacting the headteacher to request the kind of feedback which would help you with future applications.

Sometimes, interview nerves can affect the strongest of candidates resulting in a sense of failure when they did not get offered the job. At this point, when you are already working under pressure, it is all too easy to let feelings of personal rejection get a grip on you so you become locked in a state of demoralisation whenever you set about applying for another post. If this happens, you need to keep at the front of your mind that currently, somewhere between 85% and 95% of student teachers succeed in gaining first time appointments by the beginning of the new academic year. You are in a competitive market and it is not uncommon for final year students to have to attend several interviews before they get offered a position. Some students succeed in getting a full-time post as early as February, others have to wait until as late as August. It is worth remembering that all is not lost if you have not got a teaching post by May or June; others are likely to be advertised in the late summer period.

If you feel you are not getting anywhere after several interviews for posts which you believe you were strongly qualified for, it is worth getting a trusted friend or your personal tutor to talk you through your interview performance and to check your letter of application in order to try and find out where things might be improved. The act of talking things out with a sympathetic and objective listener can help restore flagging self-confidence and re-affirm the qualities and strengths which you know you possess but which can quickly recede in a pre-occupation with failure and low self-esteem. Somehow, you must continue to believe in yourself and keep applying for suitable posts. Eventually, time, patience and the law of probability will work in your favour and you will succeed in getting a job. This was certainly true for the usually up-beat and resilient Pat Grade, who experienced some despairing moments before she eventually got a post.

One of the problems for Pat was that she, like most of her mature counterparts, was limited to applications in a county which was saturated with applications from B.Ed and post-graduate finalists from two teacher training institutions. This factor, combined with a teacher market in which supply exceeded demand, made for additional difficulties, particularly for mature students with family commitments. Pat had submitted thirty applications and still had not been invited to interview. You will recall from earlier chapters that Pat had anticipated that she would eventually become the sole earner in the family because of her husband's declining health. She was understandably desperate about her financial position and began to wonder if she would have to seek employment outside the teaching profession. Her worst moment came when she did not get an interview in the school where she successfully completed her final school practice:

PG ... And the worst thing I think of all was when the school I did my final year placement in advertised for a teacher for Year 4. I didn't assume I would get the job or anything, but I thought, well, I stand a good chance here. They have seen me in action. But I didn't even get an interview. It was crushing. And the job was given to someone in my year, who I actually knew and she was very matter of fact about it all saying, 'Oh, I don't know if I will take it; I have been offered another job.' I thought, that's it, fine! I am going to be a secretary or something. Obviously, I am such rubbish! That was the worst thing. The worst thing as well was all the people in my group knew that I had been to this school and they all expected me to get the job and I didn't get the job and you almost feel embarrassed that you didn't get the job.

Pat eventually got her first interview in June and although she was not successful, she was relieved not to have been offered the post because she did not feel comfortable with the staff or the ethos of the school. By August, she was still searching but had changed her strategy by deciding to apply to education authorities where she knew there were teacher shortages. If necessary, she would exchange her rented accommodation for a similar property in an area where she could find employment. With this possibility in mind she applied for five teaching vacancies in London. Things rapidly changed for the better. Within days Pat received five written replies all inviting her for an interview. When one of the schools was difficult to reach by rail, the head offered to come and collect her in his car. Pat was subsequently offered two positions in London schools, both of which would have meant moving the family. The important issue for Pat was, that at last, a school had deemed her worthy of appointment:

PG The head said I was exactly what they wanted. I went home on cloud nine! My confidence was really boosted.

Having resigned herself to moving to London she was then offered an interview for a temporary contract in the county where she lived. With her self-esteem restored and feeling more relaxed now that she had two job offers, she went to the interview in a calm and confident state of mind. Convinced that another candidate had got the job, Pat was surprised when the headteacher asked her to return to the interview room:

PG And he said, 'Mrs Grade, can we see you?' I just sat there and smiled. And I suddenly realised he meant me! I went back and I thought this must be for the debriefing. It can't be me, they haven't offered me the job. When they offered me the job, I still couldn't believe it. And they said, 'You were so relaxed and confident and you have a very nice personality and you're very gregarious.' And it just went straight over my head. I still couldn't believe it.

Pat took up the temporary contract in January, 1995 and within a term her position was made permanent. She is now in her third year of teaching and is beginning to think about her next career move.

I have recounted the trials of Pat's struggle to get her first teaching appointment because it powerfully illustrates the importance of 'screwing your courage to the sticking place'[1] and not giving up even when your morale is at its lowest ebb. Pat had a strong teaching profile but unfortunately for her, she was having to compete in an over-supplied job market. However, her well-honed resourcefulness once more saw her through the lowest point of her training with a strategy which would have secured her a choice of two or three teaching posts, albeit at the expense of having to move the family. Once she could see some light at the end of the tunnel she was able to relax and allow her personal and professional qualities to communicate themselves at interview and she succeeded in getting a job in her home county without having to disrupt her children's schooling and family life.

The job market is now much healthier with a predicted shortfall of primary teachers for the foreseeable future. So you are unlikely to experience the difficulties which faced Pat, although teacher demand in England and Wales is likely to remain patchy with some areas in greater demand by potential teachers than others.

Whether or not you run into difficulties in the process of gaining a first appointment, the advice and guidance included in this chapter will hopefully help you to make the best of your application and interview and give you hope and encouragement when you stray onto rough ground.

Note

1   The exact quotation is, ... 'But screw your courage to the sticking place,' Macbeth, Act 1 Scene 7, William Shakespeare.

Chapter 6

The first year of teaching

'I wish', says a child in a poem by James Berry, daydreaming at the back of the classroom:

'I wish my teacher's eyes wouldn't
go past me today. I wish he'd know
know it's okay to hug me when I kick
a goal. Wish I myself wouldn't
hold back when an answer comes.'

It is a beautiful statement of what every learner requires first and foremost: to be noticed, to be attended to, to be valued, to be affirmed. Out of that attention and affirmation grow the confidence and, yes, the courage to learn: if the teacher dares to teach, that is, attend to and care for the learners, then the learner in their turn can dare to learn.[1]

You are now a graduate and qualified teacher with a class of your own. The prospect of having the main responsibility for twenty-five or thirty children's education is at once daunting and exciting. For the first time there will be no defined end to your time with the children apart from half-terms and end-of-term holidays. By and large you will be left alone to establish your authority with the children without the presence of tutors, or teachers writing observational commentaries on your teaching. It is a heady time in which feelings of dread and delight come in almost equal measure as you prepare for the new term. Endless questions flood your mind: will the first year of my teaching career be all that I expect it to be? What does it *feel* like to be a teacher in my own right? Will the children, parents and other members of staff accept and believe in me as a qualified teacher? What kind of support and advice will I be able to get now that I don't have the college or university to turn to? How will I keep abreast of all the planning and assessment for all of the children all of the time?

This chapter discusses some of the answers to these questions by drawing on the accounts of seven mature women's first year of teaching, all of whom were in their third of year of teaching when I interviewed them. Although all but one had begun on temporary contracts, they all had permanent contracts within a term or one year of their employment. Two had posts in infant school, two in junior schools, one in an independent preparatory school and one had spent three years working on a series of maternity and sick leave temporary contracts. The key issues for the women were how the first year had affected them in terms of job satisfaction and their expectations of the reality of teaching along with clearly defined landmarks which signalled their arrival as competent teachers, particularly in the eyes of parents and teacher colleagues. Their accounts give some of the flavour of the struggle and grind of their first year alongside some uplifting and rewarding periods when they could see the fruits of their efforts in a child's progress and when teacher colleagues began to ask their advice on school matters.

Feeling like a teacher: defining moments

What matters most of all to newly qualified teachers as they step into their new role, is that significant others such as pupils, parents, the head and colleague staff, will judge them as capable teachers. However nervous and unsure they may feel, they want to create an outward display of confidence and professional competence so that others will place their trust in them. To begin with, the establishment of a relationship with their first class is a top priority as is the necessary business of agreeing rules, routines and procedures for a safe and harmonious working atmosphere. All these important early encounters with a new class take up a great deal of time and energy leaving very little space for reflection as they attempt to keep on top of the everyday expectations of teaching, classroom organisation, display, lesson planning and the management of a large and diverse group of children. As is the case with most jobs in education, you are expected to hit the ground running whilst trying to give the appearance of being cool and in control. The feelings expressed by the mature women during this period were of an awesome sense of responsibility combined with a nagging fear that they would be found wanting in an area of professional judgement. The fact that the latter very seldom occurred, did not reduce the capacity for self doubt to lurk in the shadows of their minds as they grappled with the many new duties they had to learn to cope with on a daily basis. Pat Grade expressed this vividly when she described how she felt in her first few days as a classteacher:

PG You were constantly looking over your shoulder. I couldn't get rid of that feeling. ... But I was really by myself and if I chose to sit down all day and do nothing with them, nobody would find out! It was numbing. It was dreadful.

Christine Kift, who had a group of Year 4 children in an independent, preparatory school was relieved that her Head had made a decision to leave her on her own for the first few weeks so that she could learn through her own mistakes without fear of people breathing down her neck. Nonetheless, even though her headteacher had many times expressed his complete confidence in her ability, she owned to feeling terrified:

CK ... I can't actually remember very much about the first six weeks at all apart from being terrified. Absolutely terrified! And it was made worse by the fact that the school has so many traditions and rules and things that bear no relation to normal life and you have to learn all this and you were expected to know them and there I was with a class of eight-year old children coming into this boarding school and I didn't know where anything was either.

Those of you who are reading this as you embark upon your own initiation into teaching, need not be too alarmed by the reactions of Pat and Christine. The fears and anxieties expressed by most of the women in the follow-up study arose from a sense that they did not have complete control over their environment. In the first few weeks the children often know more about the school and its expectations than you do. Christine's worries were largely related to her lack of knowledge about where books and equipment were kept and where and when children were supposed to have a snack, for example. Many schools, these days, prepare a handbook for new staff which makes this kind of detail explicit. However, whilst it is undoubtedly useful to have such a book to refer to for guidelines about what to do during 'wet' playtimes for instance, you cannot assimilate all the information you need to know in advance of beginning the new term. A great deal of your learning about the workings of your school will occur as and when you need to know and more commonly, as a result of asking a more experienced teacher.

Not all the norms and routines of the school are overt and explicit, however. Some of them are so deeply embedded in the culture and history of the school that they remain hidden. Staffroom etiquette is a common area where the codes of conduct remain unspoken and implicit. New incumbents are well advised to listen, watch and wait to see what others do if they wish to avoid the censure of more experienced staff who know what they cannot yet be expected to know. These issues may seem trivial to outsiders but they are anything but trivial to a new arrival who craves acceptance and approval from her more senior peers. Pat was so conscious of being on the outside of these underlying features of staffroom behaviours and group dynamics that she shunned the staffroom altogether in the beginning:

PG I think the first thing you do without knowing that you do it, is to see the links, they are all the little groups that stick together and those who are friendly with other people and you can't talk to that person because then that person won't talk to you, sort of thing. A lot of the time I stayed out of the staffroom for the first week or two. I was too nervous to go down there because I felt I couldn't say anything because what do you know, sort of thing.

It wasn't long before Pat overcame her uncharacteristic reticence and brought a welcome hilarity and raucous laughter to the staffroom, but she learned a great deal about staff interrelationships and the culture of the school before she dared to crack her first joke.

Ann Major did not find out about an established practice in her infant school until it was too late for her to rectify the matter. Her Year 2 class was one of several classes going on a trip to the theatre just before Christmas. She had asked if there was anything she needed to take with her and was told that everything would be provided on the coach. During the interval at the theatre she discovered, to her consternation, that all the other classes were provided with drinks and there appeared to be none for her class. When she asked a nearby teacher where she could find her class's drinks she was informed that the parents always provided these and that she should have collected hers from a table in the staffroom. Ann's frustration at not having been told about this when she taken the trouble to ask if there was anything she needed to bring, and her subsequent dismay at having to tell her class that there would be no drinks until their return to school, is wholly understandable. One of the problems for new members of staff is that senior colleagues for whom the school's customs and practice have become second nature often do not realise what newcomers don't know, even when they make their ignorance about the mysteries of the school's hidden conventions abundantly clear. On the whole, it would seem that discovering the hidden culture of the school emerges through experience and the occasional error rather than through the formal channels of written and spoken communication. Whilst this would seem to be an inevitable part of the experience of being new to any organisation, be it school, hospital, office or factory, some control over the more painful collisions with its 'education' can be gained by keeping a quiet counsel and an attentive ear and eye on what others say and do, for a few weeks at least. However, if you end up by learning through error due to sublime ignorance, join the majority, take it on the chin and see it as part of the noviciate experience.

At some point during this headlong plunge into the reality of teaching an incident or event will generally occur which will test your authority as a teacher. These events can be a kind of watershed or *rite de passage* in your career which help to confirm your status: in short, they are defining moments and of key significance in your 'teacher' self-esteem. Examples of these moments were recounted animatedly by all the women in the follow-up group. For Karen James, it was the point at which she felt she had succeeded in getting her Key Stage 2 class with its history of behavioural difficulties, on her side. In Linda Vince's case, it came from the reaction of parents on parents' evening which she described as 'wonderful' because so many had warmly acknowledged the difference she had made to their children's progress in mathematics. These 'events' are worth describing in detail because they demonstrate two important issues: firstly, the significance of the support and professional respect of the headteacher in sustaining the confidence and morale of his/her new staff and secondly, the powerful impact upon the novice teacher which positive feedback from others can bring. Christine Kift was approaching Christmas and nervously anticipating her first parents' evening which she described as a 'huge landmark':

CK ... Peter (the headteacher) had very wisely not told anyone that I was newly qualified. He simply said I was a new teacher and I was treated with such immense respect. It was a complete blow, I think. I came away from that thinking, gosh, I am a teacher! Because they were talking to me and I was talking back and I was saying things and thinking somebody is going to shoot me down about this and, of course, nobody did. It was the first time I was giving my professional opinion on something and it gave me a huge boost and that then set me up for the rest of the year in school.

Parents' evenings are probably the first taste a new teacher has of the consumer's reaction to her/his teaching. This public feedback is good for the school and richly rewarding for the individual concerned. In Christine's case it not only boosted her confidence but positively affected her esteem for the rest of the year.

Pat Grade's defining moment came in the form of an individual letter from a parent asking to see her about her son's educational progress: on first reading, it appeared to question her professional competence as a teacher. The school in which she worked was in an area of relative social disadvantage, had a large number of children on the special needs register and a history of parental disputes both with the school as a whole and with individual members of staff:

PG The very first week I started, a parent wrote me a really snotty letter and demanded to come and speak to me the next day and that night I was semi-suicidal and I thought, I am rubbish, obviously the parent knows it. ... Her son is on special needs and she came in and she said to me, 'Work used to be sent home that you are not sending home.' And it clicked into place and I suddenly wasn't me anymore. I became his teacher. And I just sat there and said, 'Yes, but your child is now going to be doing this and this ...' And I just went through it all and in the end she said, 'Oh thank you so much for explaining it all to me.' And she walked out and I just went, 'Yesss!'

Given the difficulties that the school had experienced with some of their parents, Pat's success in bringing a potentially hostile interview to a satisfactory resolution was an important confirmation of her status as qualified teacher. At a very early point in the new term, she had gained enough knowledge of this particular child's learning difficulties to win the respect of an anxious parent who had started out by being critical of Pat's practice.

For others, the transition from student teacher to teacher status was more low key and relatively smooth. Indeed, Ann Major and Pamela

Jones felt that their maturity was a distinct advantage insofar because parents and children did not realise that this was their first post and they were accorded the respect normally given to more experienced teachers, from their first day onwards.

What was clear from the women's accounts of their first year of teaching was that their training had prepared them well for the toughest as well richest moments of those early nerve-racking weeks. Four out of seven of them had survived Ofsted inspections on top of all the other pressures and Helen Cornwall ended up in *two* inspections as a result of her several, temporary contracts in different schools. Interestingly, none of the women found the inspections any worse than their final teaching practices – which suggests that they probably found them less stressful than their more experienced colleagues. So however daunting and challenging this period may be, the experience of the follow-up group suggests that the professional skills and knowledge which you have acquired and practised over the years, will sustain you through the bleakest and best of times.

Making the most of your mentor

Most student teachers on the brink of their teaching career want to know what kind of professional help they can expect to receive once they leave the support networks of their college and university behind them. All newly qualified teachers working in the state sector now have an assigned mentor whose purpose is to provide them with whatever advice, help and support they need in their first year. The term, 'mentor' means an experienced and trusted adviser and the mentor allocated to you will normally be an experienced teacher who has a good knowledge of the workings of the school and who has had some form of mentorship training. Ideally, you will have someone within the same Key Stage field of expertise as yourself and, if you are lucky, someone who is working with the same or similar age group as yourself. This however, may not be possible in small, rural schools and not always manageable in larger schools, because of the particular deployment of staffing responsibilities.

The essential thing is that you have a mentor in whom you can confide and who will be sympathetic and non-judgmental about your queries and worries. To be an effective mentor requires considerable skill and sensitive judgement in knowing *what* help and information to give you as well as *when* to give it. It requires an ability to learn quickly what your strengths and weaknesses are and how you will best respond to help in developing your professional repertoire. Such a person needs to have the kind of professional credibility which makes you feel that their advice and judgement can be trusted. They also need to be well informed not only about the school, its staff relationships, children and parents but also about what support and in-service training exists outside its walls to enhance your professional development. Ideally, your mentor will possess the human qualities of insight, warmth, humour and understanding, all of which help to sustain and nourish successful adult to adult interactions. However, out there in the real world of education, things are seldom ideal. Your mentor is generally chosen for you and you may end up with a happy and instructive mentor relationship or you may find yourself having to find ways of making a less than satisfactory relationship work to your advantage.

The accounts of the women in the follow-up group revealed a varied and patchy experience of mentorship. For some, it was highly productive and beneficial; for others it was disappointing and unsatisfactory. Overall, their responses to the question of what characterised an effective mentor gave some useful insights into what mattered to them.

Linda Vince's mentor came closest to the ideal criteria. At the time Linda was working in a Middle school and in her view, the key to her mentor's success was his preparedness to build a relationship which travelled at her pace and which was finely attuned to her needs:

LV It was the relationship we built between us because he would guide me wherever necessary. He would step back; he would let me try things. He let me grow and develop at my own pace and if it was fast, he just went along with me. If I slowed down and he could see that I needed him, I was always confident that I could go and ask.

DD So there wasn't anything you felt you couldn't approach him about?

LV No, because he said to me from day one, 'Don't worry about anything. Every time you come across a bridge that you need to get across, then we will get across it together.' So he said, 'Don't worry about waiting for these things to happen, just get on and as they crop up, we'll deal with them.' And that was more practical because I didn't spend my time worrying about how do I do this, how do I do that and he would always say, 'This is the first time you have done this, Linda, I will show you how to do it.'

Knowing when to intervene, when to stand back, when to leave her to try things on her own and when to undertake new tasks with her, all helped Linda to feel secure about her work in a school which demanded very high standards and an exacting level of administrative detail on planning, recording and assessment.

Pamela Jones also spoke warmly of her mentor, who allowed her to do things in her own way without imposing a particular method or approach. Pamela was in a small, rural school, so she needed space to work things out for herself but not so much that she got into difficulties. Intervening without being intrusive and being approachable without creating a dependency relationship are perhaps of particular importance to mature students who often feel they have to cope with all but the most intractable problems before admitting to needing help.

Ann Major's mentor was a good deal younger than herself and whilst the age difference did not present problems for Ann, she believed they did for her mentor. Whilst Ann found her generally helpful, she would sometimes shrug off issues as being unimportant when they really mattered to Ann:

AM One of the things that I did find difficult with her was that she was very helpful but if I went to her on something, quite often she would say, 'Oh don't
worry about that,' and I might not have been worried but I had asked because I wanted to know. To be told not to worry about that was frustrating.
I wanted to know the answers.

Some of the school matters on which Ann wanted information may have been unimportant to her more experienced mentor, but they were of concern to Ann and, in her view, that should have been sufficient to warrant an answer. One of the difficulties for her mentor may have been that she felt uncomfortable about explaining school procedures to an older and clearly very able colleague. Whatever the reason, the age gap made Ann feel that she had to think twice about which matters she could take to her mentor if she was to avoid further stonewalling.

Two of the women did not feel they were particularly well supported by their respective mentors and that they were left to flounder and muddle through on their own when some systematic advice and professional guidance might have made all the difference to their first year. Karen James, for example, was given a mentor who only approached her twice in her first term, each time making it clear that she did not have time to be a mentor. She subsequently left the school leaving Karen without a mentor for several months. Later on Karen was given two mentors for a short period but did not feel that either was supportive:

KJ   ... I didn't like either of them; they weren't supportive. I felt that they were not particularly critical, but I didn't feel that you could go to them with a problem because they were both very close to the headteacher's way of thinking and you can't argue with that.

Karen's sense that she had no one to turn to in a time of need underlines the importance of having a mentor in whom you can confide without fear that an honest statement of current difficulties will be perceived critically or taken to the head and cited as evidence of teaching weaknesses. Karen had a difficult class which she was making progress with. What was blighting her first year was that she perceived that there was no one who could take her to the next stage in her own development and who could confirm and reassure her that what she was doing was working to the class's advantage. What also troubled her was the degree to which she felt swamped by information, the weight of which was too much for her to assimilate on top of all the other behavioural and learning difficulties she felt were top priority. What she wanted from a mentor relationship was someone with whom she could share her problems and who would help her to sift which information mattered and which could be temporarily shelved. The latter, she believed, would have helped her gain a much needed perspective on a job which was eating into too much of her personal life:

KJ   I think I would like somebody you could be honest with about how you are feeling, about feeling threatened about your professionalism and also somebody who could give you sound advice about stepping back from it a little bit because you get so into things and worrying about things. I think you need somebody to say, 'Well, actually that doesn't matter,' and you don't realise that things don't matter so desperately until you have actually gone through them. And you know, lots of worries like that, but the information that you were given was just tremendous. There is just no way you can take it in. I have sat through staff meetings not knowing a word anybody was saying.

Pat Grade also felt that her mentor merely went through the motions in terms of the role and, for the most part, left her to sink or swim. However, on reflection, she believed that being left on her own to get to grips with the organisation of her class was better for her own development and slowly emerging confidence. Fortunately, she was able to turn to a nearby colleague, who taught the same age group, for some valuable help on day-to-day classroom matters.

Whilst these reflections on mentorship are drawn from a very small group of women, they indicate a wide variation of practice. Starting your career with an effective and dependable mentor appears to be a hit and miss affair. So is there anything you can do to improve your circumstances if your experience turns out to be similar to that of Karen's or Pat's? Yes, to some extent there is. Firstly, you can often find other colleagues in the school who would be happy to discuss problems and concerns with you on an informal basis, as both Pat and Karen did. Whilst not an entirely satisfactory solution to the problem, it is better than feeling you have no one turn to in moments of anxiety or despair. Keeping in touch with former colleagues at college or university will also provide a wider perspective on matters you are not sure how to resolve. Secondly, a more proactive stance with your mentor might ensure a more productive relationship. If your mentor is not coming to see you as often as you would like, it is possible that s/he does not want to crowd you or appear to be checking up on you, preferring *you* to make the first move. This may be the case particularly with mature students who often appear to be highly efficient and capable in the eyes of other teachers. If you feel that your mentor is distant or overburdened with other responsibilities, it may help to agree a set of dates in advance for meetings to review progress or to discuss particular problems. This strategy at least ensures that you have an agreed agenda for meetings which you can both prepare for and work towards. Thirdly, if you feel that the lack of mentor support is seriously undermining your ability to succeed in the school, most headteachers would want to know about it and act to rectify the matter. A candid statement of your position with the Head may, if handled sensitively and diplomatically, move the relationship forward or prepare the ground for an alternative mentor. The reintroduction of a probationary year should reinstate structured support for beginning teachers.

Job satisfaction

Anyone reading this book will want to know how far the first year of teaching proved to be all that the women had expected and which aspects of it were most rewarding and satisfying. Teaching in a primary school is intensely demanding, with ever-increasing work loads and constant streams of new initiatives. All the women in the study had chosen teaching because they loved being on the inside of children's learning and playing a part in their educational development. It was gratifying therefore, to hear from most of them that despite the intense administrative demands which teaching was making on them, their enthusiasm and obvious delight had not been blunted. The pleasure and thrill of seeing children make progress as a direct result of their efforts was the touchstone of their work. The comments below from the follow-up group bear out the sense of challenge and deep satisfaction which they were experiencing in their day to day classroom teaching. I asked Ann Major, who had suffered from bouts of clinical depression since the latter years of her teacher training owing to the breakdown of her marriage and other personal crises, what had sustained her over the last few years:

AM Being in the classroom. That is why I wouldn't want to give it up. That has been my oasis. In the times when I have suffered from depression, everybody I have spoken to about that or have been talking to, has said how my voice, my attitude and everything changes when I talk about school.

DD Have you worked out why that is?

AM Because I like it! No, it is because I am confident in it. I know I am good at it. It sounds awful doesn't! But I know I'm good at it.

Linda Vince was asked which of the two jobs she had in teaching so far, she had enjoyed most:

LV Here I get even more pleasure. I get lots more pleasure because I feel I am doing what I was trained to do here.

DD Which is what, exactly?

LV It's the teaching and I get the reward through the children. It's wonderful!

And from Pamela Jones:

PJ It's the appreciation, not just from the children, but it's such a nice atmosphere in this school. We all seem to get on well together – not *all* the time – we're not that wonderful! We are people and we have good days and bad days but what I do, is appreciate it, and that makes all the difference in the world.

These women relished the buzz they were getting from teaching but there were other factors outside the immediate control of the women which added to their enjoyment. These included the colleagueship of working in small, year-group teaching teams where there was a unity of purpose and a sense that everybody's contribution mattered. Heads who demonstrated openly and publicly that they valued and respected their staff made new teachers feel confident that they were in the kind of supportive and professional atmosphere where they would thrive. Whilst not explicitly referred to by the women, there was sufficient inferential data to suggest that the culture and ethos of the school also played a significant part in whether or not they gained satisfaction from their work.

All the women had some form of curriculum responsibility which they were allocated in their first or second year. Pamela Jones and Pat Grade were both co-ordinators for Information Technology; Linda Vince was co-ordinator for mathematics, and Ann Major for Physical Education. Christine Kift had a cluster of responsibilities for English, mathematics and scripture but was gradually taking on more responsibility for science which had been her subject specialism at college. Karen James also had a range of subject responsibilities which included PSE (Personal and Social Education), French and Design Technology. Where these responsibilities matched the subjects the women had specialised in during their training, they provided a valuable opportunity for the women to make their mark in the overall curriculum development of the school. For the most part, curriculum leadership enhanced their work, provided opportunities for staff training in which they took a lead and contributed to their overall job satisfaction. Where this was not the case, it added an unwelcome burden to the pressures of their first year and created anxiety rather than challenge or satisfaction. Karen James was an English specialist with a particular interest in drama but, because another member of staff already occupied the English leadership position, she ended up with a range of curriculum responsibilities which neither she nor anyone else wanted. An additional frustration was that she had made it clear that she did not have sufficient expertise to provide leadership in French or Design Technology but her reluctance was disregarded on the basis that she would be well supported by other members of the staff. The promised support did not materialise and Karen's lack of expertise in any of her three allocated subjects added to her sense of isolation and professional vulnerability:

KJ   ... The French was frightening enough and I said, "I honestly don't have enough French to be able to front this," and she said, "We don't do anything on our own in this school. You'll get lots of support." Well me and another colleague just ploughed through it, basically.

DD   Did you get any support?

KJ   No. We don't get any. We are left to our own devices. In PSE, the actual teacher who was doing that was actually on secondment at the time, so I just got handed the file which meant nothing. ... But with the DT, I said to Daniel, 'What does it involve?' So he said, 'You need to order some wood!' and I said, 'What wood?'

Thus not all the women could state unequivocally that they were gaining a sense of satisfaction and pleasure from their work. Karen's negative feelings about her first year were exacerbated by the lack of any structured and regular guidance from a mentor. Apparent tensions between some of the staff and the head did not help Karen to feel that there was a collective ethos, the presence of which might have given her an anchor from which she could have worked out a clearer direction for her development. Whilst she gained considerable pleasure and reward from the progress she was making with her Year Three class, the reality of teaching fell some way short of her expectations. Two issues in particular drained her energy and dampened her enthusiasm for teaching: the relentless tide of paper-work which she felt hindered her ability to give of her best in classroom teaching and the enduring problem of motivating those children who had switched off from learning:

KJ   No, I don't think it is the job I thought it was because I think you are just so swamped with all the paperwork side of it and all the stuff that you get thrown at you that you don't have time to do the quality teaching that you like to do. ... But the way they (the children) think seems to be the hardest thing to understand, the hardest thing to get around. You can't actually change that as much as you can, perhaps, make giant leaps in helping them to learn to read. But to actually help them to understand that they are at school to learn and to make it a positive experience for them, is much harder. Maybe you learn it eventually, I don't know, but there do seem to be some children, a core of children, who, no matter what you do, no matter how interesting you make everything and the different ways you do things, they never listen. They never know what it is they have got to do next. They're not prepared to actually put any effort in and all they are interested in is when the bell is going for playtime.

I doubt that there are many teachers who would not recognise Karen's concerns and frustrations. Even the most experienced and inspirational teachers have to draw deep from the well of their expertise and teaching repertoire in order to find the key which may unlock the desire to learn in an unmotivated child. Even then, success cannot always be guaranteed. Karen might not have felt so alone with her problem had she had the benefit of effective mentorship support. As for her irritation with the encroachment of paper-work into her teaching, many of the women felt similarly, referring to it as 'a blight', 'a bind' and 'a treadmill'. However, for the most part, they found that there were sufficient compensations in their work to prevent bureaucracy becoming anything more than a burden to be expedited with the minimum of fuss. Clearly, there were insufficient compensations for Karen to make this perspective on paperwork possible.

Unless Karen is able to get the professional guidance and support she needs, it is unlikely that she will find career satisfaction in her current school. Fortunately, she had some experience of what it was like to enjoy teaching in her first, temporary appointment in a school where the headteacher placed a high priority on praising and recognising effective practice in the classroom. In the end a satisfactory resolution to Karen's difficulties might only be achieved with an alternative teaching position.

Career Development

When the women in the study first thought of applying for a course of teacher training an oft-repeated fear was that they did not have the academic ability to succeed on an undergraduate degree programme. I wrote in Chapter 1 that whilst most of them were confident about their teaching potential and ability to relate well to children , they were far less secure about their capacity to remember facts, absorb new information and analyse complex ideas. Initially, their ambitions were modest; they simply wanted to pass the course so that they could gain qualified teacher status, but they quickly proved to themselves that hard work, organisation and commitment paid off. They consistently achieved good marks for essays and assignments, showing that they *were* academically able. Three years into their teaching career, I was keen to learn how they were developing as teachers and what, if any, career plans they were contemplating. They all had plans of one kind or another, but not one expressed a desire to become a headteacher or to take on any kind of role in education which was predominantly administrative. With the exception of Helen Cornwall, who declared a speculative interest in becoming a deputy headteacher once she had secured a full-time contract, they all wanted, resolutely, to remain in the classroom where they felt they still had a great deal to learn and where the highest levels of job satisfaction were to be found. However, whilst improving their efficacy as teachers remained a central preoccupation, three wished to go further academically by reading for a Master's degree. Ann Major and Pat Grade were intending to register in the near future whilst Pamela Jones has already begun a part-time Master's Degree in Primary Education with the Open University and was considering the possibility of pursuing a doctorate in the future. For women who had initially entered higher education with trepidation and low levels of academic confidence, their current aspirations demonstrate that once academia grips their imagination and stimulates their intellect, the temple of knowledge becomes too attractive to resist. Pamela spoke enthusiastically about the positive impact of the MA course on her teaching but also admitted to her intrinsic enjoyment of study and how much she missed it once she had left college. Longer term, she expressed a wish to enter higher education as a tutor in the field of teacher training.

Beyond her intention to read for a higher degree, Ann said that she would like to have responsibility for subjects besides PE and to acquire some Key Stage 2 experience.

Pat's aspirations however, sprang from a growing disenchantment with classroom teaching. It was the first time she had experienced contact with pupils from problem home backgrounds and she had been unpleasantly surprised by the amount of truancy and social problems which affected the daily life of the classroom in her school. Her experience of teaching in this particular social context did not match the expectations she had of teaching and she was considering alternative work within education. One aspect of her work which did give her immense satisfaction was related to her responsibility as Information Technology co-ordinator. The staff at her school were not confident in this area and she had organised several training sessions with them in order to help boost their competence and skill. Her training sessions were well received and, buoyed up by her success, she was now considering becoming as advisory teacher in ICT with the Local Education Authority.

Karen James looked forward to the day when she could become an English co-ordinator. Drama was one of her specialist interests and she wanted very much to run her own training sessions in order to improve teachers' confidence and skill in an area she felt many teachers shunned. More immediately, she was keen to become a better class-teacher because, despite the difficulties she had recounted, she derived great pleasure from the progress she was beginning to make with her class. In the medium term, she hoped that she could find a teaching position closer to home.

Christine Kift was unambiguous about her wish to have more responsibility. She enjoyed administration and had relished the challenges she had been given at her preparatory school but was now considering the possibility of running her own science department in a secondary or middle school in the state sector.

Linda Vince was just beginning to make solid progress in her demanding role as mathematics co-ordinator in a large junior school. With the imminent arrival of the numeracy hour and the requirement to reach specific national targets, she felt that it would take the next five years to put her new plans for better progression and resourcing in mathematics fully into place. Beyond this she wanted to develop her skills of curriculum leadership in other subjects.

We have followed the women's journey into teaching from their first tentative steps into higher education to their eventual metamorphoses as qualified teachers. Whatever difficulties and doubts they experienced along the way, none of them regretted their decision to become teachers. It had led them on a voyage of new discoveries about themselves, about how children learn and about the knowledge which informs the complex business of teaching and learning. Their journey had changed them as people: they had become more questioning, more demanding of themselves and more confident in their professional and academic ability. Their feelings of worth and heightened self-esteem as they consolidated their success as beginning classroom practitioners sustained them when things did not go well. I have not tried to hide the moments of despair and frustration which at times overwhelmed the women as they grappled with fatigue and demanding work loads in schools which varied in their levels of support and guidance. Nor have I concealed the immense regard and respect which I have for these women whose commitment, tenacity and courage was demonstrated time and time again in the face of some daunting and debilitating personal problems. Children need and deserve teachers who have these qualities and strengths in such abundance. Teachers who have learned what it means to achieve an ambition which they believe is right for them and who refuse to give up even when things seem hopelessly bleak, are not likely to give up on children.

If the unfolding stories of the women's encounters with teacher training and the reality of classroom practice inspire others to believe that they too can achieve their aspiration to teach, then this book will have gone some way to succeeding in its purpose. However, the litmus test of how far the women believed that the peaks and troughs of their personal and professional endeavour had been ultimately worthwhile resided in the question of whether or not they would encourage other mature women to take up teaching, knowing what they now knew. This was the last question put to the women in the follow-up group and each of them responded with an unqualified, 'Yes!'

Given that so much of the advice and guidance contained in this book has been coloured and enlivened by the experiences of the women, it seems fitting to end with the words of Linda Vince as she advises a parent and a classroom assistant to take the same step she was encouraged to take, seven years ago:

LV... I can see they are hovering and they keep coming back and asking me questions about it, what did I do and everything. And I have just been very honest with them and said, once you take the big step and get there, then it becomes a way of life. You don't think anything else about it. It is just part of what you do every day. You will amaze yourself by what you can achieve that you didn't think was possible. You will underestimate yourself because you just do. You will make terrific friends who will stay with you, who will support you as you go through it together ... No, I would highly recommend it to anybody that feels as I did when I was working voluntarily in school all week, every week of the year having a wonderful time and thinking, yes, I can do this but never thinking, why don't you get your act together and do it?

Note

1   Taken from Richardson, R. (1990) *Daring to be a Teacher*. Stoke on Trent: Trentham Books, p. 97.

Appendix

The women in the study

Ruth Barker Age 34; Married; 2 children. Work experience: Laboratory technician, Mother and Toddler group organiser, Sales buyer. Father died of an industrial related illness during 1st year. Ruth suffered acute distress for much of 1st year. Graduated July, 1995, B.Ed Hons 2:2.

Pauline Cash Age 33; Married; 2 children. Work experience: Bank clerk, playgroup assistant, parent-helper. Graduated July 1995, B.Ed Hons 2:1.

Brenda Corless Age 39; Married; 2 children. Work experience: Clerk, Dental nurse, playgroup organiser, parent-helper. Graduated July, 1995, B.Ed Hons 2:2

Helen Cornwall* Age 41; Lone parent, divorced; 2 children. Work experience; Computer analyst programmer, Data control clerk, Paid classroom assistant. Graduated July 1995, B.Ed Hons 2:1. Taught for 3 years on a series of temporary, maternity and sick leave contracts. Currently searching for a full-time post. Aspirations to become a deputy headteacher.

Mary Croft Age 35; Married; 3 children. Work experience: British Horse Society Instructor, parent-helper. Graduated July1995, B.Ed Hons 2:1.

Angela Deakin Age 27; Married; 3 children. Work experience: Sales assistant, parent-helper. Mother-in-law child minded her 3 very young children but became terminally ill with cancer during Angela's 1st term. She withdrew from the course at the end of the 1st term with the intention of returning once she had found help with childcare arrangements. Has not yet returned to the course.

Sam Eves Age 39; Married; 2 children. Work experience: Tracer, parent-helper, parent-governor. Left husband during 1st term and found herself unable to gain access to her children. Became emotionally and physically ill and withdrew from the course at the end of the Autumn term as a result of ill health.

Pat Grade* Age 31; Married; 3 children. Work experience: School meals supervisor, parent-helper. Husband developed serious back problem during 1st year eventually becoming immobile. Graduated July 1995, B.Ed Hons 2:1. She is currently teaching in a junior school and has a Year 4 class. She has curriculum responsibility for ICT and is considering studying for an MA in education. Eventually hopes to become as advisory teacher for ICT.

Monica Griffiths Age 36; Married; 3 children. Work experience: Clerical officer, parent-helper. Graduated July, 1995, B.Ed Hons 2:1.

Karen James* Age 39; Married; 3 children. Work experience: Accounts clerk, Postmistress, Cub leader. Graduated July 1995, B.Ed Hons 2:1. She is currently teaching in a junior school where she has a Year 3 class. She has curriculum responsibility for PSE, French and Design Technology. She hopes to become curriculum co-ordinator for English and would like a job nearer home.

Pamela Jones* Age 35; Married; 2 children. Work experience: Accounts clerk, chemist dispenser, parent-helper. Her mother died during 1st year and her father became seriously ill. Graduated July 1995, B.Ed Hons 2:1. She is currently teaching a mixed age group of Key Stage 1 pupils at a small, rural school. She has curriculum responsibility for ICT and is currently reading for an MA in primary education. She intends to read for a PhD at some point with the intention of applying for a post as an education tutor in teacher training.

Christine Kift* Age 29; Married; 2 children. Work experience: taught drama at private school; care assistant for the elderly. Former student of Imperial College, London. Left because of ill health. Graduated July 1995, B.Ed Hons 2:1. She is now teaching a Year 4 class in an independent preparatory school where she has curriculum responsibility for English, mathematics and scripture. She would like to have more responsibility for science, her specialist subject, and hopes eventually to run a science department of her own in a Middle or Secondary school.

Beryl King Age 29; Married; 2 children. Work experience: Chemist dispenser, parent-helper. Graduated July 1995, B.Ed Hons 2:1.

Susan Krass Age 24; Unmarried; No children. Work experience: Creche leader, Playgroup leader. Safeways cashier. Graduated July 1995, B.Ed Hons 2:1.

Ann Major* Age 41; Married; 2 children. Work experience: Costs clerk, Fish and chips sales, paid classroom assistant. Separated from husband at end of 1st year. Divorced in 2nd year. Graduated July 1995, B.Ed Hons 2:1. She is now teaching in an infants school where she has curriculum responsibility for PE. She is planning to read for an MA in primary education and would like to extend her range of curriculum responsibilities. She hopes, in the future, to gain some Key Stage 2 experience.

Barbara Melling Age 34; Married; 1 child. Work experience: Manageress of restaurant; paid pianist and classroom assistant for children with special educational needs. Husband became bankrupt in 1st year was forced into redundancy and accrued serious mortgage debts. House eventually repossessed and family moved into rented accommodation. Graduated July 1995, B.Ed Hons 2:2.

Lucy Patron Age 34; Married; 2 children. Work experience: Receptionist, playgroup supervisor, parent-helper. Graduated July 1995, B.Ed Hons 2:1.

Carole Payne Age 33; Married; 3 children. Work experience: Bank clerk, Red Cross organiser, parent-helper. Husband's job moved in 2nd year and child minding arrangements became very complex. Intercalated in 2nd year with intention to return and complete the course. Not yet been able to return because of family difficulties.

Gail Prince Age 35; Married; 2 children. Work experience: School secretary and classroom assistant. Graduated July 1995, B.Ed Hons 2:1.

Marilyn Smith Age 45; Married; 2 children. Work experience: Scientific officer, parent-helper, PTA secretary. Failed final school placement and withdrew from the course at the end of the Autumn term, 1994.

Jackie Stephens Age 24; Long term relationship with live in partner; 1 child. Work experience: Section head at Sainsbury's, Sports instructor, volunteer help for autistic child. Intercalated at the end of 1st year because of financial difficulties and behaviour problems with her son. Has since returned to complete the B.Ed course.

Linda Vince* Age 39; Married; 2 children. Work experience: Accounts clerk, playgroup and parent-helper, parent governor. Graduated July 1995, B.Ed Hons 2:1. She is currently teaching a Year 6 class in a large, urban junior school. She is the school co-ordinator for mathematics and wishes to build on her work for the next five years and establish the Numeracy Hour before moving on. In the future, she would like to have curriculum responsibilities beyond mathematics.

Beth Wells Age 35; Married; 2 children. Work experience: Civil Service clerical officer, playgroup and parent-helper. Marriage broke down at the end of the 4th year. Graduated July 1995, B.Ed Hons 2:1.

Geraldine Wing Age 32; Married; 2 children. Work experience: Sales department manager, Nursery assistant. Both parents became ill during the 1st year, one eventually dying. Became very ill herself with a low, invasive lung cancer from which she slowly recovered. Graduated July 1995, B.Ed Hons 2:1.

Diane Young Age 33; Married; 1 child. Work experience: Clerk-receptionist, playgroup helper. Husband left her at the end of the 1st term. Financial problems forced her into part-time work at weekends and evenings. Graduated July 1995, B.Ed Hons 2:2.

With the exception of Susan Krass who is of Asian Indian ethnic origin, all the women in the research group are of white British origin. The age of the women recorded above indicates the age of entry to the B.Ed in 1991.

*   Denotes the seven women interviewed in the follow-up study in 1997/98 and from whom I was able to gather additional data and current employment details.

Bibliography

Acker, S. (1980) Women, the Other Academics, in Equal Opportunities Commission, *Equal Opportunities in Higher Education* Report of an EOC/SRHE Conference at Manchester Polytechnic, Manchester, EOC.

Becker, H.S.(1952) 'Social Class Variations in Teacher Pupil Relationships,' *Journal of Educational Sociology,* Vol 25, pp.451-465.

Becker, H.S., Geer, B., Hughes, E.C. (1961) *Boys in White. Student Culture in Medical School.* The University of Chicago Press.

Bird, E. and West, J. (1987) 'Interrupted Lives: A Study of Women Returners', in Allatt, P. *et al.* (Eds) *Women and the Life Cycle: Transitions and Turning Points.* Basingstoke: Macmillan: pp.178-91.

Burgess, H. (1989) 'A Sort of Career: Women in Primary Schools', in Skelton, C. Ed) *Whatever Happens to Little Women? Gender and Primary Schooling.* Milton Keynes: Open University Press: pp.79-91.

Burgess, R.G. (1982) 'The Unstructured Interview as a Conversation', in Burgess, R.G. (Ed) *Field Research: A Sourcebook and Field Manual.* London: Unwin Hyman: pp.107-110.

Cooley, C. (1902) *Human Nature and The Social Order*, 1983 edn. New Jersey: Transaction Books.

Coser, R.L. (with L.Coser) (1974) 'The housewife and her greedy family', in Coser, L. *Greedy Institutions: Patterns of Undivided Commitment.* New York: Free Press.

Coulby, D. and Bash, L. (1991) *Contradiction And Conflict. The 1988 Education Act in Action.* London: Cassell Educational.

Duncan, D.M. (1995) *Mature Women Entrants To Teaching: A Case Study.* Unpublished PhD Thesis, University of Warwick.

Edwards, R. (1993) *Mature Women Students: Separating or Connecting Family and Education.* London: Taylor and Francis.

Epstein, C. (1983) *Women in Law.* New York: Doubleday.

Fairbairn, G.J. and Winch, C. (1991) *Reading, Writing And Reasoning: A guide for students.* Milton Keynes: SRHE and Open University Press.

Goleman, D. (1996) *Emotional Intelligence: Why it Matters More than IQ.* London: Bloomsbury Paperbacks.

Lacey, C. (1977) *The Socialisation of Teachers*. Series: Contemporary Sociology of the School. London: Methuen.

Lorber, J. (1984) *Women in Medicine*. London: Tavistock.

Lortie, D.C. (1975) *School Teacher: A Sociological Study.* Chicago: University of Chicago Press.

Mead, G.H. (1934) *Mind, Self and Society.* Chicago: University of Chicago Press.

Miller, C. and Partlett, M. (1974) *Up to the Mark.* London: Society for Research into Higher Education.

Nias, J. (1989) *Primary Teachers Talking: A Study of Teaching As Work*. London: Routledge.

Pascall, G. and Cox, R. (1993) *Women Returning to Higher Education*. Milton Keynes: The Society for Research into Higher Education and Open University Press.

Pollard, A. (1982) 'A Model of Classroom Coping Strategies', *British Journal of Sociology of Education*, 3,1. pp.19-37.

Richardson, R. (1990) *Daring to be a Teacher*. Stoke on Trent: Trentham Books.

Richardson, R. (1996) *Fortunes and Fables: Education for Hope in Troubled Times*: Stoke on Trent: Trentham Books.

Teacher Training Agency (1998) *The Use of Resources in Partnership: A Working Paper.* London: TTA.

Whiteside, T., Bernbaum, G., and Noble, G. (1969) 'Aspirations, Reality Shock and Entry into Teaching', *Sociological Review*, 17,3, pp.399-414.

Some Suggested Further reading

Comer, T. (1996) *Opportunities For Mathematics in the Primary School*. Stoke on Trent: Trentham Books.

Lockwood, M. (1996) Opportunities for English in the Primary School. Stoke on Trent: Trentham Books.

Peacock, A. (1997) *Opportunities for Science in the Primary School*. Stoke on Trent: Trentham Books.

Sedgwick, F. (1989) *Here Comes The Assembly Man: A Year in Life of a Primary School*. London: The Falmer Press.

Index